GOVERNMENT AND POLITICS OF WYOMING

Third Edition

Government and Politics of Wyoming

JOHN B. RICHARD
Professor of Political Science
University of Wyoming

KENDALL/HUNT PUBLISHING COMPANY
DUBUQUE, IOWA

Copyright © 1966, 1969, 1974 by John B. Richard

Library of Congress Catalog Card Number: 73—94197

ISBN 0—8403—0228—2

All rights reserved. No part of this publication may be reproduced, stored in a retrieval system, or transmitted, in any form or by any means, electronic, mechanical, photocopying, recording, or otherwise, without the prior written permission of the copyright owner.

Printed in the United States of America

Contents

Preface vii

Chapter		Page
1.	The Wyoming Political System	1
	The System and Its Boundaries	2
	Federalism	5
	The State Constitution	14
2.	Wyoming Political Parties, Elections, and Interest Groups . . .	19
	Voting Preferences and Political Parties	19
	Nominations and Elections in Wyoming	29
	Interest Groups and Politics	31
3.	The State Legislature, Politics, and Legislation	41
	Legislative Powers and Limitations	41
	Apportionment and Representation	44
	Social Backgrounds of Wyoming Legislators	49
	Legislative Structure and Organization	53
	The Legislative Process	56
4.	The Governor, Politics, and Administration	61
	The Office of Governor	61
	The Roles of the Governor	63
	Divided Administration	73
5.	The State Judicial System	77
	The Role of the Courts	77
	Jurisdiction of State Courts	79
	Organization of the Wyoming Courts	80
	The Judicial Process	83
	Selection of Judges	85
	Law Enforcement	87
6.	Local Government	89
	Legal Status of Local Governments	90
	Municipal Government	91
	County Government	96
	Special Districts	98

Preface

State and local governments are becoming increasingly important in the total governmental system of the United States. Such factors as the national government's preoccupation with Vietnam for so many years, the Mideast crisis, the energy shortage, Watergate, sheer size of the national government, all contribute to a resurgence of state and local governments in many areas of governmental policy. The national government is too taken up with these factors to perform satisfactorily on such a wide range of activities. If the local and state governments of our nation are to respond to this challenge and remain vital parts of our political system it is imperative that citizens be knowledgeable about the lower levels of government.

In this third edition we have made some considerable changes in several areas and only minor revisions in other portions. Three major constitutional changes were approved by the voters in the election of 1972 including Municipal Home Rule, a change in the process for selection of judges, and annual sessions for the state legislature. These we have attempted to describe briefly. In addition the new revenue sharing program for state, county, and municipal governments is also discussed. It should be noted again, however, that the primary purpose of this book is to provide minimal information about state and local governments in Wyoming and it is intended primarily for use as supplementary reading in political science courses on American and Wyoming governments. Those readers who might expect a complete or definitive work on the political institutions and affairs of this state will be disappointed.

I would like to acknowledge the help of many people in the preparation of this text. Several members of the Political Science Department at the University of Wyoming and several graduate students helped considerably and I appreciate it.

Laramie, Wyoming   John B. Richard

CHAPTER ONE

The Wyoming Political System

State government is the pivot point of the governmental system in the United States. The states acting collectively created the national government; individually they established local governmental structures. Traditionally they have performed vital governmental services required by citizens. Despite the tremendous and important role that state governments play in the lives of every citizen of this country, little attention has been given to their affairs. On the one hand, the national government is involved in gigantic and interesting, varied and frustrating, dangerous and complex programs throughout the world, about which the average citizen knows something. In addition, many citizens are at least vaguely aware of local governmental and community projects since they usually cannot escape them or their impact. Somewhere in between these two levels of government, national and local, lies the state government, about which the average citizen knows little and is dubious or critical at best. Perhaps the states merit the distrust and disinterest of citizens. Former North Carolina Governor Terry Sanford, in his study of state governments points up this problem vividly: "In fact, the states are their own worst enemies. No state can be strong with a weak legislature, a hamstrung chief executive, a harassed judiciary, a chaotic administrative structure, an invidious interest group atmosphere, weak political parties or public apathy. Through the years, most states have been infected with a hold-the-line attitude that positions them too often between the people and their needs. In the public mind, states' rights extremists too often have seemed to have been the only spokesmen, thus confirming the public image of the states as bottlenecks to progressive action."[1]

Yet the governments and politics of our states merit concern by citizens. It is in the state political arena that most of the vital domestic programs are actually determined or implemented. The states also have a crucial part in administering many national programs. Problems in education, highways, public health, regulation of business, law enforcement, elections, conservation, pollution, civil and criminal law, operation of prisons, parole and probation, mental health programs, to name just a few, are usually settled, if not solved, in the individual states. Still, it would seem that state political arrangements and governmental structures are seldom the objects of concern by the citizenry and when they are, their concern is about a very vague and general notion of "states' rights" and increasing "encroachment" of the national government. State politics tend to be viewed as tax politics or restrictive politics rather than program-oriented as in the national government. Few state citizens or even politicians seem to worry about whether the state is exercising efficiently and constructively the powers and duties it already has.

The states really are the pivot points in the larger national political system and have crucial and vital roles to play. Programmatically, in a country the size of ours, from the standpoints of both area and population, the national government simply could not singlehandedly carry out many, if any, domestic programs. As a result few functions are now strictly national or state or local projects alone. Accomplishment of governmental goals requires joint and cooperative efforts by all three levels of government—national, state, and local. Politically, the major political parties are largely coalitions of state and locally-based parties. United States senators and representatives are predominately local officials because of the election system used in this country, and even the president seeks election through the electoral college in which votes are allotted to and captured in the individual states.

THE SYSTEM AND ITS BOUNDARIES

Broadly speaking, government is the mechanism through which authoritative rules of behavior for the society are determined and implemented. Government, however, is more than just a mechanism, it is a political process in which every individual and organization is involved whether actively demanding changes or merely passively supporting the status quo. In a sense, government and politics include all human behavior designed to influence the making of public policy and its enforcement, whether the activity or behavior is by a single individual, political party, interest group, or official agency of the formal structure of government.

At some time or another, nearly every individual or group in society acts in a political way. Individuals and groups, however, are usually only part-time politicians in the sense that their political acts are only small segments of their total social behavior and relationships. We will take the view that political activities, however, can be analytically abstracted from general social activities, and do in fact comprise a unified political system. The term "political system" has been used with increasing frequency by political scientists as a useful analytical tool for pointing out the interrelatedness and interdependence of political behavior.[2]

Political system suggests that there are differentiated and identifiable political units, activities, or sets of interactions which comprise an identifiable whole, with boundaries that distinguish the system from its environment. Further, all the elements, units, or parts of the system are closely interrelated and interdependent, in that, activity in one segment of the system affects, and in turn is affected by, activities in other sections of the whole. Every part has a certain relationship to the whole and stress or change in one segment affects the larger system.

It is possible, therefore, to speak of the Wyoming state political system. It is generally similar to the political system in each of the other forty-nine states since they all began with roughly the same political tradition and operate within the same larger national political system. The Wyoming political system might include by way of example, individual citizens acting in a political way, interest groups, political parties, the press, three branches of government—executive, legislative, and judicial—all of which may interact and become interdependent within the system at any given moment in time. Decision-making authorities within the system such as the executive, legislature, or courts, receive demands for action, or support for present policies from the environment and these decision-making centers respond to the demands and/or support by rewarding or depriving differentially the participants in the system. If certain individuals or groups receive advantages from the system they may be completely satisfied or they may seek more advantages. Those who receive disadvantages may seek to rectify their situation. This is the principle of feedback, whereby decisions made by the decision-making authorities feed back into the system in the form of new demands or new support of the system. These influences and stresses which enter the political system from the environment, the actions taken on the influences or response of the system, and the subsequent return to the system through feedback comprise the whole dynamic concept we call the political system.

Every political system has stresses placed on it by the environment within which it operates. An extremely important problem then which must always be considered in analysis of a system is that of the boundaries to the system: boundaries necessarily having to be identified in order to distinguish the political system from that which is not to be included—the environment. The Wyoming political system is demarcated in a number of ways. There is, of course, the geographic boundary of the state. With some exceptions, the state may not act or operate outside of its legal geographic limits. The physical environment including natural resources, climate, topography, aridity, and similar properties of the state influence to a large extent the types of political problems that are likely to be fed into the political system. Indeed the biological makeup of the citizenry can and does influence or create uncertainties for the political system.

Probably the most obvious part of the environmental system which strains the political system is the social system, which here, for purposes of simplification, will include not only the social structure, but cultural and economic aspects which influence the political system. Mere demographic characteristics of the population of Wyoming place certain kinds of stresses upon the political system and not others. The social system in Mississippi, for example, is not entirely similar to that which exists in Wyoming and therefore different types of stresses from outside the political system determine the kinds of problems with which the system will have to cope. The stresses of urban blight and congestion do not plague the Wyoming political system as they do in certain metropolitan areas of the country.

Wrapped up in every social system is a certain culture which influences social action. Culture here may be taken to mean those meanings, symbols, and values which influence the patterns of social action in a society. We are concerned particularly with the political culture and its influence on the ways in which political roles are played. We are also interested in the ways in which political culture is transmitted from generation to generation in what we might call political socialization. What traditions, heroes, symbols, values, institutions, styles, among other things, influence or stress the political system?

Recently the Midwest Research Institute completed an extensive study on the quality of life in the various states and regions of the nation. This study concentrated on nine goals established by President Eisenhower's Commission on National Goals and attempted to measure by virtue of 91 different indicators a social-economic-political index and ranking of the states. Wyoming ranked almost exactly in the middle (24th) of the fifty states. The goals included such measures as "democratic process" which included the building of an informed and involved citizenry, improving the quality of public administration, and increasing the collaboration and sharing of power among all levels of government. Indicators of accomplishment of this goal included percentage of total population of voting age casting ballots, median salaries of government employees, freedom of local governments to solve their own problems, among others. Wyoming ranked 35th in terms of its "democratic process." Other goals, with Wyoming's rank among the fifty states in terms of accomplishment of these goals, included: status of the individual, 17th; equality, 15th; education, 11th; economic growth, 43rd; technology change, 46th; agriculture, 5th; living conditions, 28th; and health and welfare, 32nd.[3] Thus, it should be seen from this brief discussion that there are certain factors outside the political system which may affect that system and its operation.

There are also at least three other important boundaries which limit the activities of the state political system: the state constitution; the federal system; and, local governments operating within the state. The state constitution, as a boundary to the political system, sets the legal limits within which political decision-makers must operate. The federal arrangement is such that the state political system is only part of a larger three-level operation which affects what the state can accomplish. Finally, there are many local units of government operating within the state. Technically, these sub-units are subject to legal direction by the state in a unitary governmental arrangement. In fact, however, they play a vital role in policymaking and operate outside of the daily supervision and direction of state-level officials.

The remainder of this chapter will discuss two of these important boundaries of the state political system: the federal arrangement and the state constitution.

Local governments and their involvement in the state political system will be dealt with in a later chapter.

FEDERALISM

State political systems do not exist in a vacuum—they are part of the larger political system in the United States. They exist in a federal system. Federalism, in a legal sense, denotes a system of government in which governmental powers are divided between a central government and areal governments, each having some functions to perform but neither receiving its power from the other. The division and distribution of functions and powers between the central government and the regional governments are based upon a common set of rules or constitution which cannot be altered individually by either of the levels nor even by the ordinary legislative, administrative, or judicial processes of both levels.

In the United States, according to this constitutional distribution of powers, the national government has those powers and functions which are expressly assigned to it by the Constitution, and those which can be reasonably implied from the express provisions of the Constitution. The states, on the other hand, according to the Tenth Amendment, have all those powers not delegated to the national government. A number of powers, however, are expressly denied to the states by national Constitution as well as by their own individual constitutions. The national government as well is denied certain powers by the Constitution, while both levels have certain powers and functions which are performed concurrently. In case of conflict between levels of government and to make this system operable, the constitution provides that the national Constitution, laws, and treaties are the "supreme law of the land," "anything in the Constitution or laws of any State to the contrary notwithstanding."[4]

It is clear from the above that the Constitution does not clearly define the term federalism. It delegates certain powers to the national government and reserves the rest to the states. The delegated powers are, however, to be interpreted to include certain implied powers and the national courts are the referees of the federal system in case of conflict. There are also some other constitutional provisions which spell out certain relationships between the national government and the states and relationships of states with other states. The national government is obligated to guarantee every state a "republican" form of government, to protect the states from invasion and domestic violence when they request it, and to prohibit the involuntary dismemberment of a state without its consent. Exactly what constitutes a republican form of government has never really been determined since the Supreme Court has indicated this is a "political" question to be decided by the political branches of government, namely the President and Congress. The question of protection against domestic violence upon application by the state has been involved in a number of recent riots and disturbances in several areas of the country. The question of carving up a state is probably of historical interest rather than a pressing current issue.

In addition to obligations of the national government to the states, states have constitutional obligations toward one another. Article IV of the constitution provides that each state give "full faith and credit" and recognize as valid all records, public acts, and judicial proceedings of other states although there are some noteworthy exceptions. In addition, Article IV provides that the "privileges and immunities" of citizens of each state are to be granted to citizens of the United States hopefully precluding discrimination against nonresidents. Again, there are notable exceptions. Finally, extradition is provided for in the constitution, namely that a governor is supposed to return an individual apprehended in his state to the state where the alleged criminal activity took place upon the request of the governor of the state where the crime took place. Clearly many governors do not feel bound by this even though the language seems mandatory.

This legal set of relationships in the Constitution does not, however, specify in detail all possible divisions of power between the two levels of government, nor does it necessarily describe either the historical or present-day patterns of intergovernmental relationships among all levels of government. The constitutional federal structure has served historically as a *means* for dividing and sharing the functions and powers of government, rather than as an *end* to be achieved in the allocation and specification of particular powers and functions for particular levels of government. Citizens make certain demands for services and functions to be performed by government as opposed to private enterprise, and the federal system—national, state, and local—is a response to these demands. Contemporary political activities are far too complex and interdependent to be labeled as "federal" or "local" in this difficult time. One level of government simply could not manage all governmental affairs. Thus, while modern government is far different than that which existed at the beginning of our country, the basic attributes of the federal structure as outlined in the Constitution are essentially the same as they were then, namely, a means to achieve governmental objectives rather than an end to be achieved in itself.

Local governmental units, although not a part of the legal federal structure, also are vitally involved in the federal system if it is viewed as a means of sharing governmental functions. The local unit of government, legally a subdivision of the state in a unitary system of government, nevertheless performs a vital role in the sharing of governmental functions along with the states and the national government.

Functions of government, then, both because of the Constitution and despite it, are not discretely allotted to particular levels of government to the exclusion of other levels—they are shared functions.[5] Frequently all levels of government are involved in a single function of government. No one jurisdictional unit acts entirely on its own, but each governmental activity is part of a larger sphere of action involving other levels of government. In recent years several attempts have been made to "turn back" to the states certain functions and to remove the national government from these functions. These efforts have been largely failures, not because the ideal is not good, but because this sort of response does not represent the way in which governments today operate. Governments, in other words, in a political world of scarce resources, integrate and share resources and powers. This is sometimes in government text books referred to as "cooperative federalism." We choose not to use this particular phraseology because it seems to imply that all levels of government cooperate and get along. The concept of sharing does not necessarily imply that at all but tries to indicate that there is a mutuality of interest in certain social and political matters and government-in-action as opposed to government-in-theory is a matter of shared concern which might include considerable conflict as well as cooperation. It is in this sense that the term "federal" is used in this section, rather than in the strictly legal sense of specific division of power between the state and national governments. Federalism then is a means to achieve general governmental objectives, not an end to be achieved in itself.

This conception of federalism, often characterized as being introduced and fostered by the New Deal or by the system of monetary grants-in-aid, is not necessarily only a phenomenon of recent years, nor even of this century. The tremendous expansion of activities by the national government in recent years did not create an "enforced" cooperation nor did it impose situations that did not exist in some form previously. Although total governmental activity by all levels of government has increased, the patterns of sharing and techniques of cooperation have existed since the beginning of the system. Daniel Elazar, in his study of 19th century federalism, found that the techniques of sharing and cooperation were in use all through the 19th century, long before the relatively recent advent of the monetary grant-in-aid.[6] Even if the monetary grant-in-aid is used as an indicator of the existence of federalism as a sharing device, it will be shown later, at least in the case of Wyoming, that the role of this device has been of significant impact since the beginning of statehood and is not a phenomenon of relatively recent vintage.

The present-day system of sharing under the federal system is an enormously complex process of providing necessary services and regulations by government to the population of all jurisdictional units. Expansion of activities at all levels of government has taken place generally throughout the nation's history; but in the last thirty years government's role in general, and the national government's role in particular, have been expanded in both service and regulatory activities. This is not to say that sharing of activities has decreased, but on the contrary that more areas of mutual concern to all levels of government have been created.

Grants-in-aid

The federal system of sharing takes a variety of forms, including the grant-in-aid and various collaborative administrative devices and techniques used by officials of different levels of government. The grant-in-aid is the most obvious device illustrating the system of sharing. The national government with its advantages of size and availability of resources, monetary and otherwise, makes vast sums of money available to states and local governments to accomplish specified purposes. The size and scope of grants-in-aid have increased tremendously in recent years to the point where many critics feel that the presence of increasing aid actually endangers the autonomy and independence of local units of government. Actually, the amount of grants-in-aid relative to total state revenues in Wyoming has increased only negligibly in the last thirty years. (See Table 1.) State expenditures, in other words, have also increased tremendously. The grant-in-aid therefore has remained about the same, percentagewise, in relation to total state revenue. Relatively speaking, the federal grant had actually increased very little by 1971 as compared with 1932 before the advent of the so-called New Deal, which is so often suggested as the

TABLE 1
State Revenue and Federal Payments in Wyoming,
1892-1971 (Dollar Amounts in Thousands)

Year	Total State Revenue	State Revenue Excluding Federal Aid		Federal Payments		
		Amount	% Increase	Amount	% Increase	% Total State Revenue
1892	$ 217.6	$ 185.0		$ 32.6		15.0
1898	255.8	225.4	21.8	30.4	−6.7	11.9
1902[1]	459.0	417.7	85.3	41.3	35.8	9.0
1907[1]	811.8	740.2	77.2	71.6	73.3	8.8
1912[1]	1,220.2	1,114.2	50.5	106.0	48.0	8.7
1916[1]	1,937.5	1,814.0	62.7	123.5	16.5	6.4
1922[1]	10,621.1	8,318.1	358.5	2,303.0	1,764.8	21.7
1927[1]	11,910.1	8,795.2	5.7	3,114.9	35.2	26.2
1932	10,487.0	6,530.0	−25.7	3,957.0	27.0	37.7
1937	14,010.0	8,379.0	28.3	5,631.0	42.3	40.2
1942	17,664.0	13,688.0	63.4	3,976.0	−29.4	22.5
1947	20,017.0	14,750.0	7.8	5,267.0	32.5	26.3
1952	59,877.0	41,924.0	184.2	17,953.0	240.8	29.9
1957	84,236.0	57,933.0	38.2	26,303.0	46.5	31.2
1962	124,516.0	76,176.0	31.5	48,340.0	83.7	38.8
1967	165,874.0	96,175.0	26.3	69,699.0	44.2	42.0
1971	246,000.0	158,000.0	63.5	82,900.0	18.9	33.7

1. Computed by dividing figures for biennium by two. Source: *Biennial Reports of the Treasurer of the State of Wyoming,* and Bureau of the Census, *Compendium of State Government Finances* in 1967, 1962, 1957, 1952, 1947, 1942, 1937, Washington, D.C.: U.S. Government Printing Office.

beginning of a new brand of federalism. The major advances in the grant-in-aid program were made prior to 1932 with the Federal Highway Program in 1916 and the Mineral Leasing Act in 1920, which returned a percentage of the mineral royalties received by the national government from its mineral holdings to the state in which the lands were located.

In Wyoming, there seems to be a significantly lesser amount of opposition to these latter two programs, highways and mineral leasing grants, by most people than to many of the other programs. Together these two programs constitute about 70% of intergovernmental revenue available to the state of Wyoming from the national government. If these two programs are omitted from consideration the remainder of the national grants-in-aid make up less than 10 per cent of the total revenue available to the state from all sources.

The fact that the grant-in-aid seems to have remained a relatively stable portion of state revenue, however, tends to obscure another tremendously significant item, in that the number of grants-in-aid has increased tremendously in recent years. Because of the pressures by various groups and interests in Congress, the number and scope of national activities have increased tremendously in recent years. Depending upon how finely we break down the federal aid programs there may be as many as 1100 separate federal aid programs administered by nearly 100 agencies.

Revenue Sharing

A key feature of the "new federalism" as defined by President Richard Nixon has been the widely heralded general revenue sharing passed by Congress and signed into law by the president in October, 1972. Under the State and Local Fiscal Assistance Act of 1972 over $30 billion in national tax revenue is to be "shared" with the many general purpose governmental units in the United States over the next five years. The first revenue sharing checks were distributed in late 1972 and early 1973 and governmental units have been authorizing the expenditures of funds since that time. First proposed by Professor Walter Heller of the University of Minnesota, revenue sharing has been discussed in Congress since 1958, but not until President Nixon's request to Congress in 1969 and final passage in 1972 did it become a reality.

The primary argument for revenue sharing centered around the fact that state and local governments had inadequate resources to meet state and local needs. The national government, although it had provided an increasing number of categorical grants-in-aid programs, had the advantage of taxing income and could provide the necessary funds to meet the general problem of the fiscal inadequacy of the state and local governments. The categorical grants-in-aid programs which usually required matching monies and with "strings" attached, it was alleged, were responsible for the transfer of policy making authority in many areas from state and local governments to the national government. In addition, state and local budgets were often distorted by the matching requirements leaving the local governments with little money to finance its real priorities.

President Nixon's proposal provided for an automatic distribution over a five-year period. The distribution of the funds in Wyoming and every state was based on a set formula of one-third to the state and two-thirds to various local units of government in the state. No strings were attached to the use of the money at the state level and only general limits were placed on local uses. Finally, all general purpose local government (municipalities and counties) are eligible for the revenue sharing money. See Table 2. The amount the State of Wyoming receives including both state and local shares is based on three factors: population, tax effort by the unit of government, and income per capita.

While there are no so-called "strings" attached to the uses of revenue sharing monies at the state level, the act lists "priority expenditure" areas for which local shares must be spent. These priority areas include: (a) public safety including law enforcement, fire protection, and building code enforcement; (b) environmental protection including sewage disposal, sanitation, and pollution abatement; (c) public transportation including transit systems and streets and roads; (d) health; (e) recreation; (f) libraries; (g) social services for the poor and aged; (h) financial administration. Expenditures on these priority areas can include operating expenses as well as capital expenditures. These broad purposes include most of the policy areas in which local governments are involved and consequently the limitations are not significant. As a matter of fact it is apparent that local governments could use the money for nearly any purpose by a simple "juggling" of the books although this is not encouraged by the national government. Even though it is not encouraged there is no legal way in which it could be prevented. Further prohibitions in the act are that the money cannot be used as matching for categorical grants from the national government and discrimination on the basis of race, color, creed is prohibited.

What are the advantages of the revenue sharing arrangement? Most observers think that it will provide revenues for programs and projects which local leaders and citizens feel are important. There are few strings attached in contrast to the categorical grant program. Local governments do not have to apply for revenue sharing funds; they come automatically based on a general formula. Administrative and accounting procedures are simplified and the local governments can concentrate on the programs instead of monitoring federal programs. Since decisions are made at the local level concerning the use of the funds revenue sharing might increase citizens' awareness of local problems and solutions. Naturally there are opponents to the concept of revenue sharing. The primary argument used against it is that Congress has abdicated control over national money to irresponsible and irresponsive local governments. In addition efficiency would suffer and probably categorical grant programs would decline particularly in the social concerns category. It is difficult to assess the full impact of this important program at this early date however.

TABLE 2
Total Revenue Sharing Money to the Cities, Counties, and State of Wyoming January 1, 1972 Through December 31, 1976

	Entitlement I	Entitlement II	Entitlement III	Received to 6-30-73	Total of All Entitlements
State of Wyoming	$1,627,000	$1,578,000	$1,831,000	$ 5,036,000	$18,542,000
Counties:					
Albany	250,837	239,451	282,320	772,608	2,859,187
Big Horn	127,208	121,356	143,174	391,738	1,449,990
Campbell	180,238	172,232	202,860	555,330	2,054,461
Carbon	192,926	184,416	217,141	594,483	2,199,089
Converse	85,564	81,766	96,304	263,634	975,313
Crook	65,719	62,849	73,967	202,535	749,100
Fremont	321,435	306,977	361,779	990,191	3,663,913
Goshen	93,372	89,313	105,092	287,777	1,064,315
Hot Springs	69,297	66,176	77,795	213,268	789,892
Johnson	54,006	51,549	60,785	166,340	615,597
Laramie	325,665	310,931	366,540	1,003,136	3,712,122
Lincoln	101,506	96,996	114,246	312,748	1,157,025
Natrona	375,388	360,219	432,422	1,168,029	4,835,772
Niobrara	42,294	40,303	47,603	130,200	482,094
Park	165,598	158,061	186,382	510,041	1,887,583
Platte	70,924	67,794	79,826	218,544	808,434
Sheridan	114,845	109,815	129,259	353,919	1,309,070
Sublette	45,873	43,720	51,630	141,223	522,886
Sweetwater	265,477	253,540	298,798	817,815	3,026,066
Teton	25,702	24,605	28,928	79,235	292,965
Uinta	60,188	57,457	67,742	185,387	686,057
Washakie	109,314	104,472	123,034	336,820	1,246,027
Weston	61,164	58,381	68,841	188,386	697,182
County Total	$3,253,395	$3,107,530	$3,661,735	$10,022,660	$37,084,139
Grand Total*	$4,880,397	$4,880,397	$5,492,603	$15,253,397	$55,626,180
Selected Cities:					
Casper	$ 181,364	$ 173,296	$ 204,127	$ 558,787	$ 2,067,293
Cheyenne	125,381	119,729	141,118	386,225	1,429,167
Laramie	80,268	76,507	90,342	247,117	914,940
Rock Springs	32,123	30,541	36,155	98,818	366,154
Sheridan	52,714	50,419	59,330	162,463	600,863

*Totals may not agree due to rounding
Source: Wyoming Taxpayers Association, *Newsletter,* June 19, 1973, p. 3.

Administrative Techniques of Sharing

Besides the grant-in-aid program there are numerous other ways in which the three levels of government share programs and activities in certain fields of endeavor. In almost every area of governmental concern there are cooperative arrangements and administrative techniques of sharing which do not necessarily involve an exchange of funds. The state engineer, for example, has participated in a program of stream gauging under a cooperative agreement with the Surface Water Branch of the U.S. Geological Survey since 1915, and since 1940 he has participated in a cooperative program of ground water investigations. The U.S. Geological Survey, the state engineer, and the water planning program also cooperate in investigations of the quality of Wyoming waters.

The state game and fish department has worked very closely with national agencies for many years on numerous projects. Much of the fish and game resources are located on public lands administered by national agencies such as the Forest Service and Bureau of Land Management, and it is the responsibility of the state agency to manage and develop the habitats and fishery resources of these areas as well as state and private areas. Many cooperative programs over the years have developed ad hoc and on a permanent basis, such as periodic conferences, cooperative personnel training schools, and meetings attended by both state and national officers each year. In addition a number of specific cooperative programs have developed. A recent example occurred on the Green River in western Wyoming. In 1962 the state game and fish departments of Wyoming and Utah, with financial and personnel aid from the national agencies, completed a fish rehabilitation program on the Green River fishery. The game and fish department has also cooperated with national agencies in providing access to prime hunting and fishing areas through construction of roads or facilities in a number of areas.

In the management of state and private forest lands the state forester of the state board of land commissioners has engaged in a number of cooperative programs and agreements with other state, local, and national agencies. Of primary concern are fire suppression programs on forested and nonforested watershed lands. The University of Wyoming's program in extension and experiment farms is, of course, an extremely good example of multi-agency, multi-level sharing.

Another indicator of the involvement of all levels of government in various areas of endeavor is the number of public employees in the state. Total public employment in the state since World War II indicates that all levels of government are directly involved in a great number of functions with the state and local employment figures rising considerably while that of the national government has remained relatively stable since 1947. This would seem to indicate that state and local governments are expanding their endeavors at a much faster rate employment-wise than the national government. It also seems to indicate that, in terms of the national government's employment of personnel in the state, Wyoming is not being "invaded" by increasing numbers of "bureaucrats" as is so often pointed out by some state officials. See Table 3.

TABLE 3
Wyoming Public Employment
Federal, State, Local
1952, 1972

	1952		1972	
	No.	%	No.	%
Federal	5,969	35.1	5,335	19.0
State	3,206	18.8	7,166	25.6
Local	7,846	46.1	15,485	55.3

Source: U.S. Bureau of the Census, Public Employment in 1972 (1952), Series GE 72, No. 1, Washington, D.C.: Government Printing Office, 1972.

Local and state employment increased significantly between 1952 and 1972 across the board both in terms of type of government employment and function performed. County employment rose from 1,594 to 3,549; municipalities from 1,566 to 1,897; school districts from 4,399 to 9,672; and special districts from 287 to 367. By function, the numbers of education employees rose from 5,501 in 1952 to 12,005 in 1972; highways from 1,087 to 1,944; public welfare 185 to 584; health and hospitals from 417 to 2,916; police and fire from 618 to 1,082; etc.[9]

Thus far it has been suggested that state government's activity does not take place in a state vacuum unaffected by outside forces. State administrators and politicians operate in a vast governmental network of associations among all levels of government. Many inter-level programs have been adopted and advanced. In the modern age especially, with a premium placed on professionalization, skill, and education, programs have been advanced by governmental officials almost regardless of the particular level with which affiliated.

Administrators, however, who have constant contact with professionals in their fields at all levels of government tend to view the national-state relationships with mixed feelings. In other words, while the federal system may be a sharing arrangement, this does not inevitably rule out the possibility of conflict between and among levels. Sharing does not involve cooperation only, but rather both possibilities—cooperation and conflict. It would seem that the very nature of the sharing process induces conflict in certain types of relationships. Individual agencies at the three levels of government tend to compete with one another on occasion, each unit seeking to maintain its own autonomy and prevent other units or groups from modifying its goals and activities. As resources, material and symbolic, become scarce because of expanding population and economic activities, competition among units of government also increases, resulting in conflict among the units, each seeking to maintain its own position, often at the expense of others. One area of conflict, for example, has concerned the respective legal positions of the state and national governments in the exercise of jurisdiction over water resources. Periodically, in the last 100 years, questions concerning the relative legal positions of the respective levels of government in water resource allocation and development have arisen.[10]

THE STATE CONSTITUTION

Basically a constitution determines the general structure of the governmental system and specifies the rights of citizens. A constitution is the "higher law" of the system and is beyond the reach of ordinary legislative and administrative policy-making processes. Each of the state constitutions sets the basic legal limitations to the political system, generally defining the boundaries of political activity. State constitutions, however, are subordinate to the national Constitution and must conform to the Constitution, laws, and treaties of the United States. The national Constitution also specifically limits state political activities in a number of other detailed instances. In this section, however, we shall be concerned primarily with the state constitution and boundaries that it imposes on the state political system.

Generally speaking the state constitution can be broken down into five major subdivisions: (1) bill of rights; (2) structure of government; (3) other or miscellaneous matters; (4) amending process; and, (5) schedule. In actuality the Wyoming constitution has 21 different articles of varying importance and length. Much of the content of the state constitution will not be discussed in detail here, but will be mentioned in subsequent chapters.

Every state constitution has a bill of rights which specifies certain freedoms of the citizens of that state. The Wyoming Declaration of Rights (Article I) contains 37 specific sections, some of which contain more than one guarantee. Many of these provisions are copied from the national Constitution, but Wyoming founding fathers apparently deemed it wise to take extra precautions specifically forbidding certain governmental activities. Since states have reserved powers, it probably seemed necessary to specify safeguards against legislative, administrative, and judicial abuses of authority.

A few general points about the civil liberties guaranteed by the state constitution should be noted. First, the Declaration of Rights contains a number of what might be called general principles rather than particular individual rights. Some examples of these statements of principle are: "Power is inherent in the people" (Sec. 1); "all members of the human race are equal" (Sec. 2); "equal political rights regardless of race, color, or sex" (Sec. 3); "absolute, arbitrary power over lives, liberty and property exists nowhere in a republic, not even in the largest majority" (Sec. 7); "military power is subordinate to civilian authority" (Sec. 25); "all laws of a general nature shall have a uniform operation" (Sec. 34); "any rights not enumerated are retained by the people" (Sec. 36).

Second, there are many particular civil and political rights that people in Wyoming enjoy. Some examples of these rights are: no imprisonment for debt (Sec. 5); freedom of religion (Sec. 18); freedom of speech (Sec. 20); right of petition (Sec. 21); rights of labor protected (Sec. 22); right to the opportunity for education (Sec. 23); right to bear arms (Sec. 24); free and open elections (Sec. 27); private property may not be taken for public use without just compensation (Sec. 33). There are also other specific rights listed.

Finally, the Declaration of Rights provides that "no person shall be deprived of life, liberty or property without due process of law" (Sec. 6). It lists certain substantive guarantees such as prohibiting ex post facto laws (Sec. 35) and a specific definition of treason (Sec. 26). Also it lists numerous procedural rights which may be construed by the court to afford due process of law to the people of Wyoming, including: no unreasonable search and seizure (Sec. 4); right to defense counsel (Sec. 10); courts open to everyone (Sec. 8); trial by jury (Sec. 9); no self-incrimination (Sec. 11); no double jeopardy (Sec. 12); no excessive bail (Sec. 13); no suspension of habeas corpus (Sec. 17); and others. The due process clause, of course, is subject to repeated reinterpretation by the courts. In other words, due process of law might be defined as "anything that is not unreasonable as determined by the courts."

The second major category of the state constitution contains provisions generally describing the structure of state government. These structural provisions are found largely in Articles II, III, IV, and V. Article II declares that the powers of government shall be divided among three departments—legislative, executive, and judicial—and Articles III, IV, and V specify the appropriate officials, qualifications for office, selection and removal processes, terms of office, and powers and duties of the three branches of government. Each of these branches will be discussed in subsequent chapters.

The third major section of the Wyoming constitution contains the largest bulk of the constitutional provisions. Suffrage, education, irrigation and water rights, mines and mining, corporations, state boundaries, county government, municipal corporations, salaries, taxation and revenue, public indebtedness, state militia, public lands and donations, and a "miscellaneous" article comprise this segment of the constitution. Some of these matters are discussed later and others are outside the scope of this book. All, in a sense, place limits on the operation of the political system.

The fourth major section of the constitution contains the procedure for amending or changing the state constitution (Article XX). The present state constitution has been amended 39 times since 1890. Actually, of course, the meaning and general tenor of the constitution might be changed other than by the formal process of amendment. Custom and usage, statutory elaboration, and judicial interpretation over the years have probably changed the meaning of the constitution more than the 39 formal changes in the wording.

The first step in the formal amending process is the proposal. A proposed amendment may be submitted in either house of the legislature and if it is approved by two-thirds of all the members of each house, it is submitted to the voters. The second or ratification stage occurs when the proposed amendment is submitted to the voters for approval or rejection. The proposed amendment is approved when and if "a majority of the electors shall ratify the same" at a general election. The Wyoming Supreme Court has interpreted this to mean a majority of all voters participating in the election rather than just a majority of voters voting on the issue. Since constitutional amendments are on a separate ballot and citizens rarely understand or indicate an interest in issues, many ballots are not used. People failing to vote or refusing to vote on the constitutional issue in actuality are voting "no" on the issue since a majority of all participating voters is required.

The constitution also provides for amending or changing the constitution through use of a constitutional convention. This technique has never been permitted by the legislature, however. If two-thirds of the elected members of each house in the legislature propose the calling of a constitutional convention, the issue is submitted to the people. If a majority of all voters participating in the election favor calling a constitutional convention, at its next session the legislature must provide for calling the convention. When and if the constitutional convention meets and when and if it writes a new constitution, the proposed new constitution would have to be approved by the voters.

The final segment of the state constitution has little, if any, contemporary significance. It is the Schedule and provides for the orderly transition from territorial to state government. It specifies the necessary steps to be undertaken in order that the new constitution might be put into operation.

There are many criticisms that might be made concerning the constitution. It is far too long and should be confined to fundamental principles as is the case in the national Constitution. In many instances the constitution is not only detailed but inflexible and contains many items that would be better regulated through more easily-changed statutes. Because of the length and detail frequent changes are often necessary and voters have neither time nor interest to consider lengthy amendments and constitutional issues. While these criticisms are often voiced, it is not likely that significant constitutional changes will occur in the near future. Vested interests are always determined to maintain their permanent access points, guaranteed and legitimized by the present state constitution.

FOOTNOTES

1. Terry Sanford, "A New Strategy for State Initiative," Speech delivered at the 72nd Annual Conference of the National Municipal League, November 15, 1966, p. 2.
2. David Easton, *A Framework for Political Analysis*, Englewood Cliffs, N.J.: Prentice-Hall, Inc., 1965; Herbert Jacob and Kenneth Vines (editors), *Politics in the American States: A Comparative Analysis*, Boston: Little, Brown and Company, 1965, Chapter 1.
3. John O. Wilson, "The S-E-P Index: How Does Your State Rank?" *State Government Administration*, November 1968, pp. 12-13.
4. *United States Constitution*, Article VI.
5. Morton Grodzins, "The Federal System," in President's Commission on National Goals, *Goals for Americans*, New York: The American Assembly, Columbia University, 1960, p. 266.
6. Daniel J. Elazar, *The American Partnership: Intergovernmental Cooperation in the Nineteenth Century United States*, Chicago: University of Chicago Press, 1962.
7. *Biennial Report of the Wyoming Department of Public Health*, 1951-1952, p. 7; 1953-1954 p. x; 1959-1960, p. 36.
8. *Wyoming Wildlife*, Vol. XVII, No. 11, November, 1953, p. 9; *Annual Report of the Wyoming Game and Fish Commission*, 1961, p. 101.
9. Bureau of the Census, *State Distribution of Public Employment in 1972*, Washington, D.C.: U.S. Government Printing Office, 1972.
10. See John B. Richard, *State Administration and Water Resources in Wyoming* (unpublished Ph.D. Dissertation, University of Illinois Library, 1965.)

CHAPTER TWO

Wyoming Political Parties, Elections, and Interest Groups

The basic unit of political behavior is the individual person. Elections are collective actions of many individuals which determine not only who shall hold office, but place limits on the activities of the legislators and administrators in our political system. It is absolutely essential then that we look briefly at certain institutional devices which determine periodically who the political leaders will be.

There are many ways for citizens of Wyoming to participate in politics. They might write letters to their congressmen or state legislators; donate money to a political party; go to political rallies, dinners, or speeches; lick stamps or stuff envelopes for a political party; belong to interest groups which are actively supporting or promoting a particular policy or goal; or simply express their political preferences in a voting booth. Most citizens, however, are only part-time politicians, participating only when they deem it convenient or necessary. This chapter will be primarily concerned with some of the more important tangible features of political participation: voting and the general nature of support for political parties; organization of political parties; primary and general elections of governmental officials; and interest groups and their supporters in the state.

VOTING PREFERENCES AND POLITICAL PARTIES

Generally, it might be said that the United States has a two-party political system. This is not to say, however, that the two parties are therefore equally strong in all areas of the country. In some areas, only one major party exists for all practical purposes. In other areas one party is so dominant in terms of winning offices and votes, that the second existing party is rarely in a position to capture governmental offices. In other areas, both parties seem to have relatively equal opportunities for capturing political prizes of government. In other words, it seems that we do not have a full-blown, nationwide two-party system, but rather each major party is actually a loose federation of many local and state parties of varying sizes, strengths, and shapes.

What seems to be true of the national party system, might also be true of political parties in Wyoming. At the state level it seems reasonable to say that there exists a two-party system with each party in a position to win the major political offices on occasion. The Republican party in this state has been far more successful historically, but the Democratic party regularly contests vigorously most state-wide offices and usually has a good chance of winning some of the major offices. Table 4 illustrates this picture of two-party politics in Wyoming with the Republicans slightly dominant. In elections for national offices, Wyoming could be classified as a "doubtful state" having voted for the winning presidential candidate in every election since statehood except in 1944 and 1960. When Democrats captured the presidency, however, the state was not as Democratic, precentagewise, as the nation.

But what is true in the state-wide picture is not necessarily true in each of the several counties in the state. The Republican party is not equal in strength to the Democratic party in Sweetwater county, nor is the Democratic party equal in strength to the Republican party in the extreme northern tier of counties in Wyoming. On the other hand, Laramie county is one of the national "bellweather" counties—one of only five or six nationwide that has voted for the winning presidential candidate every single time since 1900. This bellweather status is borne out in our analysis of elections in which the county appears as an uncertain one for either party (see Table 5). Just as the national political parties are loose federations of state parties of varying degrees of strength and organization, so are the states relative to local parties. This section will deal first with the relative voting strengths of the two political parties in Wyoming and then turn to a brief discussion of party organization.

Voting Patterns and Preferences

An extremely large majority of the voters generally expresses a definite preference for one or the other of the two political parties and these preferences are very stable over the lifetimes of individuals. This means that the true "independent," one who weighs studiously the candidates' qualifications and issues in each election before making up his mind on the best candidate or issue position, for all practical purposes, exists in such small numbers as to be relatively insignificant except in very close elections. Political scientists have conducted a number of voting studies which indicate the predominance of party identification as a predictor of how an individual will vote and have closely correlated particular party identifications to a number of demographic characteristics such as age, education, sex, locale, religion, occupation, etc. Such voting survey studies, however, have not been conducted in Wyoming. Therefore, it is necessary that we make some broad assumptions about the voting behavior of Wyoming citizens based only on aggregate data from election statistics.

As mentioned earlier, Wyoming is definitely a two-party state although two strong parties do not seem to exist in all sections of the state. Generally, it has been said that the northern, more rural counties have been largely Republican

TABLE 4
Party Affiliation of Successful Candidates for National, State Elective Offices, and State Legislature, in Wyoming, 1890-1968

Year	President	U.S. Senate	U.S. House	Governor	Secretary of State	State Auditor	State Treasurer	Supt. of Pub. Inst.	Senate Dem.	Senate Rep.	Senate % Rep.	House Dem.	House Rep.	House % Rep.	Repub. % Popular Vote for President
1890		R R	R R	R	R	R	R	R	3	13	81.3	7	26	78.8	
1892	D		D D						5	11	68.8	16	12[1]	36.4	
1894		R R	R R	R	R	R	R	R	4	14	77.8	2	34[1]	91.9	
1896	D		D						4	14[1]	73.7	11	23[1]	60.5	
1898		R	R R	R	R	R	R	R	6	13	68.4	3	35	92.1	
1900	R	R	R						2	16[1]	84.2	2	34[1]	85.0	58.8
1902			R R	R	R	R	R	R	2	21	91.3	4	46	92.0	
1904	R		R R	R R			R		3	20	87.0	3	47	94.0	69.6
1906		R	R R	R	R	R	R	R	2	21	91.3	5	45	90.0	
1908	R		R						3	24	88.9	7	49	87.5	58.3
1910		R	R D	D	R	R	R	D	6	21	77.8	25	31	55.4	
1912	D	R		R					8	19	70.4	28	29	50.9	48.7[2]
1914			R D	D	R	R	R	R	9	18	66.7	15	42	73.7	
1916	D	D		R					11	16	59.3	25	32	56.1	43.4
1918		R	R R	R R	R	R	R	R	10	17	63.0	11	43	79.6	
1920	R		R						3	22	88.0	1	53	98.1	66.8
1922		D	R D	R	R	R	R	R	5	20	80.0	23	37	61.7	
1924	R	R		R D					11	16	59.3	23	39	62.9	76.5[3]
1926			R R	R	R	R	R	R	12	15	55.6	17	45	72.6	
1928	R	D		R					10	17	63.0	11	51	82.3	64.3
1930		R	R R	R	R	R	R	R	6	21	77.8	26	36	58.1	
1932	D		R D						12	15	55.6	42	20	32.3	42.1
1934		D	D D	D	D	D	D	D	14	13	48.1	38	18	32.1	
1936	D	D		D					16	11	40.8	38	18	32.1	38.2
1938			R R	D	D	R	R	R	11	16	59.3	19	37	66.0	
1940	D	D		D					11	16	59.3	28	28	50.0	47.0
1942		R	R D	R	D	R	R	R	10	17	63.0	17	39	69.6	
1944	R		R						6	21	77.8	20	36	64.3	51.2
1946		D	R D	R	R	R	R	R	7	20	74.1	10	46	82.1	
1948	D	D		R					9	18	66.7	28	28	50.0	47.8
1950			R R	R	R	R	R	R	10	17	63.0	17	39	69.6	
1952	R	R		R				R	6	21	77.8	11	45	80.4	62.8
1954		D	R R	R	R	R	R	D	8	19	70.4	24	32	57.1	
1956	R		R						11	16	59.3	26	30	53.6	52.1
1958		D	R D	D	R	R	R	D	11	16	59.3	30	26	46.4	
1960	R	R		R					10	17	63.0	21	35	62.4	55.1
1962		R	R R	R	R	R	R	R	11	16	59.3	19	37	66.0	
1964	D	D		D					12	13	52.0	34	27	44.2	43.4
1966		R	R R	R	R	R	R	R	12	18	60.0	27	34	55.7	
1968	R		R						12	18	60.0	16	45	73.8	55.7[4]
1970		D	D R	R	R	R	R	R	11	19	63.3	20	40	65.5[1]	
1972	R	R		D					13	17	56.7	17	44	70.9[1]	69.4

[1] In 1896 and 1900 there was one third-party member in the Wyoming Senate. In the House of Representatives there were 5 third-party members in 1892, 1 in 1894, 4 in 1896, 4 in 1900, 1 in 1970, and 1 in 1972.
[2] Represents only 34.7 per cent of total popular vote.
[3] Represents only 51 per cent of total popular vote.
[4] Represents percentage of 3-party vote. Wallace received 8.7 per cent of the total vote and Humphrey 35.5 per cent.

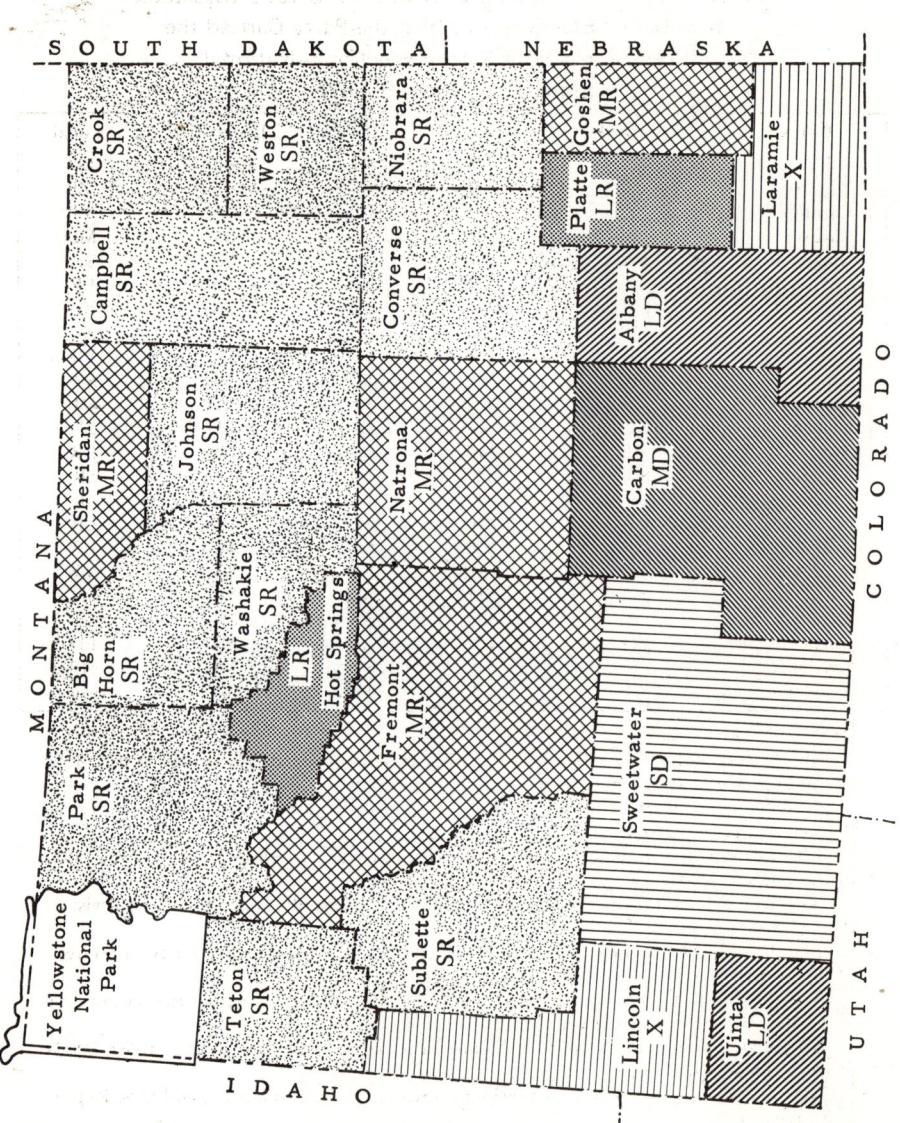

Figure 1. Political map of Wyoming.

TABLE 5
Party Success in Wyoming Counties, 1948-1972 (Based on Number of Elections in which the Party Carried the County, for Four Sets of Elections—National, State, Legislative, County)

County	Composite	National	State	Legislative	Local
Albany	LD	LD	LR	MD	LD
Big Horn	SR	SR	SR	SR	MR
Campbell	SR	SR	SR	LR	MR
Carbon	MD	MD	SD	SD	MD
Converse	SR	SR	SR	SR	SR
Crook	SR	SR	SR	MR	LR
Fremont	MR	SR	SR	SR	X
Goshen	MR	SR	SR	MR	X
Hot Springs	LR	MR	SR	X	LD
Johnson	SR	SR	SR	SR	SR
Laramie	X	X	LR	LD	MR
Lincoln	X	MR	LR	LD	LD
Natrona	MR	MR	SR	MR	LR
Niobrara	SR	SR	SR	SR	SR
Park	SR	SR	SR	SR	SR
Platte	LR	MR	MR	LR	LR
Sheridan	MR	MR	MR	MR	LR
Sublette	SR	SR	SR	SR	MR
Sweetwater	SD	SD	SD	SD	SD
Teton	SR	SR	SR	SR	SR
Uinta	LD	LD	LD	MD	LD
Washakie	SR	SR	SR	MR	MR
Weston	SR	SR	SR	SR	MR

KEY:

SR—Strong Republican County—Republican party carried the county in 85-100% of the contested offices.

MR—Moderately Republican County—Republican party carried the county in 70-84% of the contested offices.

LR—Leaning Republican County—Republican party carried the county in 56-69% of the contested offices.

X—Divided County—the two parties split the contested offices by closer division than 55% to 45%.

LD—Leaning Democratic County—Democratic party carried the county in 56-69% of the contested offices.

MD—Moderately Democratic County—Democratic party carried the county in 70-84% of the contested offices.

SD—Strong Democratic County—Democratic party carried the county in 85-100% of the contested offices.

National Elections—offices of Presidential electors, U.S. Senators, and U.S. Representatives.

State Elections—Governor, Secretary of State, Auditor, Treasurer, Superintendent of Public Instruction.

Legislative Elections—State Senators and Representatives.

Local Elections—Ten local offices at county level.

and the southern tier of counties along the Union Pacific railroad has been largely Democratic. Although Wyoming is a "doubtful" state, the situation in certain counties is more or less predetermined. Sweetwater county is extremely strong in its support of Democrats at all levels and several northern counties have been equally strong for the Republican party. One measure of the strengths of the two parties is their relative success in carrying each county in contests for national, state, legislative, and local offices.

Table 5 shows that the two parties have not been equally successful in all areas of the state. According to the criteria for classification mentioned in the table, eleven counties are designated as Strong Republican counties, indicating that 85-100 per cent of all the contested offices were won by Republicans between 1948 and 1972. In Johnson county, for example, not one single Democrat succeeded in obtaining a majority of county voters for any office at any level of government. Four counties were classified as Moderately Republican indicating that 70-84 per cent of the offices were won by Republicans in that county. Two counties were classified as Leaning Republican. Thus, 17 counties can be classified on the Republican side of the ledger in terms of the long run preferences of the voters residing in those counties.

On the Democratic side only one county was classified as Strong Democratic. In Sweetwater county only four Republicans have been able to carry that county in 182 contests over a period of twenty years. One county was classified as Moderately Democratic, and two were designated as Leaning Democratic. Two counties, Lincoln and Laramie, were classified as evenly divided in which neither party was clearly dominant in the long run for all levels of elections. In Laramie county overall, the Democrats won 51.1 per cent of the contested elections, making it impossible to put this county clearly on the Democratic list of counties. As indicated earlier, Laramie county is classified as a national bellweather county, never having voted "wrong" for president since 1900 through the 1972 election.

Although Table 5 indicates that voters in many counties are remarkably consistent in their voting preferences for the various offices at different levels, in some counties voting behavior in national or state elections is considerably different than that for legislative or local offices. In Hot Springs county, for example, Republican candidates at the national and state level have fared extremely well, while for local offices Hot Springs voters apparently prefer Democrats. In several other counties it should be noted, that local and legislative elections are considerably different from state and national patterns. In addition to Hot Springs county, discrepancies between local or legislative contests and state or national preferences can be noted in the following counties: Albany, Crook, Fremont, Goshen, Laramie and Lincoln. In other counties, Natrona, Sheridan, and Platte, there are less significant discrepancies, although some differences exist. This would suggest that Wyoming voters are fairly sophisti-

parties, elections, and groups

cated in their choices for the several levels of political offices, apparently splitting tickets rather consistently in some counties. In other counties it is apparent that straight-party ticket voting is the case.

This appraisal of party strength in each county, however, only tells how many offices were won by a party, but does not tell us how large the margin of victory was. Professor Karsch, in his analysis of party strengths in Missouri counties, uses a "strength in depth" measure—a party's percentage of the total vote cast in the county for several offices.[1] This was also done for the 1966 state election in Wyoming counties. See Table 6. The figure for each county is the Republican percentage of total vote cast in all seven major state-wide races in 1966: United States Senator, United States Representative, Governor, Secretary of State, State Auditor, State Treasurer, Superintendent of Public Instruction. Table 6 shows that the Republicans have a decided advantage in most counties and that while Democrats have some surface strength in certain counties for particular offices, their strength in state-wide races is rather shallow. It should also be noted in the table that there is a very close correlation between the number of offices captured by each party and the relative strength in depth of the party in each county. Under either measure of party strength the first twelve counties in the Republican camp are the same, although in different order. The Democratic counties are also the same under both measures, surface strength and strength in depth.

Although these data do not prove the fact, they support the idea that the parties are decentralized, with little, if any, connection between the state and local parties. The data suggest also that state legislative politics seem to be of a different variety than either state politics or local politics, although the exact nature of the differences is not readily discernible.

What else might be said about the nature of the Republican and Democratic strengths in the various counties? Are Strong Republican counties different from Strong Democratic counties? In order to make some general assumptions about politics in Wyoming, and to suggest some possible answers to these questions, several social and economic characteristics of the population in each county were compared with the party classification scheme.

Democratic strengths, with exceptions, are probably associated with the number of urban dwellers in a county. On the other side of the picture, Republican strengths, with some exceptions, are generally correlated with the percentage of the labor force in the county that is employed in agriculture. It is clear, however, that the population of the state is relatively homogeneous and that there are not significant differences between Republicans and Democrats in terms of income, housing, and education. It must be remembered, however, that gross population data were being used and some actual differences might exist that were not shown by the gross data.

TABLE 6
Party Success in Wyoming Counties, 1948-1972 Compared with Republican Percentage of County Vote in Seven State-wide Races Combined, 1966

County	Per Cent of Offices Captured by Republicans 1948-1972[1]	County	Republican Per Cent of Popular Vote, 1966[2]
Johnson	98.5	Crook	75
Teton	97.8	Johnson	75
Park	96.3	Niobrara	75
Niobrara	95.8	Sublette	74
Converse	93.9	Teton	70
Sublette	92.2	Campbell	68
Big Horn	90.7	Converse	68
Weston	88.6	Park	67
Washakie	86.1	Weston	65
Campbell	86.1	Big Horn	65
Crook	85.7	Washakie	64
Goshen	77.3	Goshen	60
Fremont	76.9	Sheridan	60
Sheridan	76.1	Fremont	58
Natrona	71.5	Lincoln	58
Platte	65.5	Platte	56
Hot Springs	60.9	Hot Springs	56
Lincoln	49.4	Natrona	54
Laramie	48.9	Albany	50
Albany	41.4	Uinta	50
Uinta	33.8	Laramie	48
Carbon	18.1	Carbon	46
Sweetwater	2.2	Sweetwater	34

[1] Taken from Table 5, based on the number of elections in which the Republican Party carried the county for four sets of elections: national, state, legislative, county.

[2] Figure for each county is the Republican percentage of the total vote cast in that county in all seven state-wide races in 1966: U.S. Senator, U.S. Representative, Governor, Secretary of State, State Auditor, State Treasurer, and State Superintendent of Public Instruction.

Source: Secretary of State, *Wyoming Official Directory and Election Returns* (1948-1972).

Finally, we should make some mention of the number of people who participate in elections in Wyoming. While it is difficult to say exactly how many people in Wyoming meet the basic voter qualifications, there are probably about 220,000 potential voters in the state. Approximately 165,000 voters are registered to vote with roughly 45% registered as Republicans, 40% as Democrats, and 15% as Independents. Between 70% and 80% of the registered voters normally participate in an election. In 1966 87% of the registered voters participated and in 1968 90% of the registered voters actually cast their ballot. Smaller percentages participated in 1970 and 1972.

This percentage is considerably higher than is the case in most of the rest of the United States. In presidential elections about 60-65% of the eligible electorate can be expected to participate in an election. This usually drops considerably in off-year elections.

Not all voters, however, vote for every office listed on the ballot in any given election and this represents another important voting pattern that should be mentioned. For example, of the 128,978 voters who went to the polls in 1968, only 127,205 voted for President; 123,313 voted in the Congressional race; 111,400 indicated for Supreme Court Judge; and only 106,329 and 96,308 voters made a choice on the two amendments listed on the ballot. This same pattern could be noted in the 1970 election for the various state offices. Thus, it would appear that not all races on the ballot interest all the voters and as one descends the ballot the number of people voting tends to get smaller and smaller.

Party Organization

The legal definition of political party in Wyoming is "a party which at the last preceding election cast for its candidate for representative in the Congress of the United States at least ten (10) per cent of the total vote cast at such election for such office."[2] This legal definition does not, however, describe the basic functions of political parties in our society which are to nominate and elect candidates to political office with aspirations of achieving some measure of control over governmental structure and policy.[3] From this specification of basic party functions, it seems evident that there are really two forms of party organization, that which exists outside the governmental structure and engages in nominations and campaigns, and that inside the government controlling personnel and policy.

Extragovernmental Party Organization. The Wyoming legislature has passed a great deal of legislation defining the extragovernmental organizational structure and functions of political parties in Wyoming.[4] (See Figure 2.) At the lowest level is the precinct organization. In the primaries of the respective parties, voters of each party select one precinct committeeman and one precinct committeewoman. Precinct officers, although legally at the bottom of the organizational hierarchy, occupy probably the most significant positions in the whole organization. It is the precinct officer who is responsible for the real work in the party, contacting members of his party, getting potential voters registered to vote, and insuring that voters are present at the polls on election day. Apathetic or lazy precinct committee members can defeat a party since this is the primary basis for direct contact with voters by the party organization.

The next level of organization in the party is the county central committee, which consists of the precinct committeemen and committeewomen of each party in each county. Precinct committee members who reside within incorporated cities and towns also constitute the city central committee of each

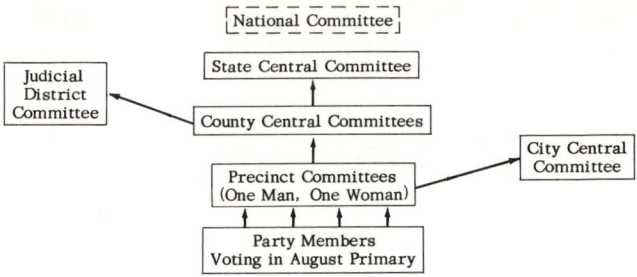

Figure 2. Political party organization in Wyoming.

political party. The county central committees each biennium select county chairmen who are responsible for guiding and coordinating, but not necessarily controlling, the activities of precinct committee members of the party in the county. The county central committee also selects one state committeeman and one committeewoman to represent the county party in the state level organization. Members of the state central committee residing within the limits of a judicial district constitute the judicial district committee of the party.

The state central committee of each party obviously is composed of one man and one woman from each county. This committee must select a state chairman, who in turn is responsible for attempting to coordinate and guide the party's work at the state level.

Superimposed on these organizational structures of the two political parties are conventions at both the county and state levels. Every two years each party in each county must hold a convention. At the state level a convention in each party is also held at which time state party platforms are drawn up, and in presidential election years delegates to the respective national conventions are chosen, presidential electors for the party are selected, and national committeemen and committeewomen are selected.

This seemingly highly structured party organization is, however, largely a paper organization. The party is not a neat hierarchical system with clear lines of authority and responsibility from top to bottom. The informal power of many strong private individuals and government officeholders in the party who do not hold party organizational positions, make authority and responsibility in the party somewhat meaningless terms. In other words, again, the two parties are largely decentralized in terms of political power and in terms of organizational structure.

Intra-governmental Party Organization. The political parties of Wyoming are largely oriented toward winning elections and have not subsequently followed up with strong intra-governmental party programs. Through control of various administrative offices and legislative positions, the parties have a significant amount of political patronage, but this does not always mean that a clear-cut party organization exists in government, at least not to the degree that is found in some states and in the national Congress and Presidency.

In terms of control of the state government, the Republican party has been clearly dominant. In the legislative branch the Republicans have controlled both houses of the legislature in all but five sessions (ten years). The Democrats have controlled both houses in only two biennial periods during the 1930's. (See Chapter Three.) Similarly in the administrative branch, the Republicans have controlled all five of the elective offices 40 years during the 84-year history of the state, while the Democrats captured all five major offices only one four-year period during the 1930's. (See Chapter Four.) On the state boards and commissions, the Democrats have controlled a majority of the five offices for a period of ten years, the Republicans having a majority 26 years. The Republicans, thus, have controlled all or a majority of the five offices for a total of 58 years, and one two-year period was evenly divided after a gubernatorial resignation. Only five of 20 Secretaries of State, three of 20 State Auditors, four of 20 Superintendents of Public Instruction, and one of 22 State Treasurers have been members of the Democratic party.

NOMINATIONS AND ELECTIONS IN WYOMING

Choosing officers of government by the election process is a difficult task when one considers that there are many millions who are technically eligible for the literally thousands of offices of government. The election process, therefore, is divided into two separate steps: (1) nomination; and (2) election. The first stage in the process is a boiling down stage, eliminating all but a few candidates (usually two for each office) from consideration so that the second stage will be more meaningful and will result in a majority vote for the ultimate winner.

Nominations in Wyoming

For all practical purposes the nomination process is a party affair in which candidates whom the party will support in the final election are selected. Methods of nomination have varied in the past but the usual form today is through the direct primary. Historically, the parties have used the local caucus, the legislative caucus, and the convention system for nominating candidates, but each of these forms came in for criticism because of the alleged likelihood of machine control and manipulation. Since the middle of the last century, at the local level and almost exclusively at all levels in this century, except for the presidency and vice-presidency, nominations are made by the direct primary. In this system eligible voters are able to choose for their party the candidate they feel will best represent the party. This democratization of the nomination process has also been criticized considerably in that it often saddles the party with a candidate whom the party leaders and workers cannot support wholeheartedly in the final election, but this system is likely to be maintained.

There are actually four major forms of direct primary in the United States: closed primary, open primary, blanket primary, and nonpartisan primary. In Wyoming, at least for partisan offices, the closed primary is used as it is in all but about a dozen states. In the closed primary the voter must declare his party allegiance or affiliation and upon doing so he is given only the ballot of that party.[5] In the open primary the voter receives ballots for all the parties in the election without making a commitment for one or another of the parties. Once in the voting booth the voter may choose one of the party ballots and vote it, discarding the others. In the blanket primary the voter is allowed to vote for candidates of either party as long as he doesn't vote for two candidates of different parties for the same office. This type of primary is used only in the state of Washington. Wyoming and most other states, also use the nonpartisan primary for selecting candidates for nonpartisan offices such as judges, city council, or county superintendents of schools.

Closed primaries seem to be preferred by party officials because only party members can vote and it seems to protect the integrity of the party. In the open primary the voter can choose in secrecy which of the party ballots he prefers and party leaders complain that such a system facilitates "raiding" by members of the opposition party thus insuring weak candidates for one's own party. Charges of raiding, however, are difficult to prove and it is unlikely that much of this actually occurs.

Wyoming's primary election occurs biennially in August before the general November election. After the primary is over a party candidate for each office that has received the largest number of votes is declared to be that party's candidate in the general election. It might be noted here that a majority is not necessary in order to win the party nomination and in a number of primary elections majorities are not received by the winning candidates. When many candidates vie for a particular office within one party the winning candidate often will receive only a plurality of votes from party members, yet he represents the party in the general election.

Elections

Nowhere in the world are there as many elections and as many officers of government selected via the election process as in the United States. Wyoming generally follows this prolific pattern of electing numerous officials of government. In Wyoming voters select electors for president and vice-president, two U.S. senators, one U.S. representative, governor, secretary of state, state auditor, state treasurer, state superintendent of public instruction, 61 state representatives, 30 senators, five supreme court judges, 11 district judges, clerk, treasurer, assessor, sheriff, attorney, coroner, clerk of district court, and three commissioners in each county, plus mayors, city councilmen, and officers and board members of special districts.

Qualification for Voting. Every state, including Wyoming, has certain requirements that must be fulfilled in order to vote. These usually are age, citizenship, residence, and literacy. In Wyoming a voter must be a citizen of the United States and Wyoming; 18 years of age; resident in the state and county 30 days; and be able to read the constitution of Wyoming.[6] It might also be noted that Wyoming was the first state in the union to grant equal voting rights to women. There are also some restrictions on who may vote: "No person shall be a qualified elector who is an idiot or insane person, or who has been convicted of an infamous crime. . . ."[7] Although the statutes claim that it is not a prerequisite to voting, registration of voters is generally required in the more populated areas of Wyoming. Each county clerk and municipal or town clerk in the state is a registration official. The voter must appear before one of these registrars and swear that he meets the necessary qualifications for voting. Registration is permanent in this state if the individual continues to vote, although his name is removed from the registration list if he does not participate in one general election.[8]

Ballots. Wyoming uses the general system of balloting known as the Australian ballot. It is secret, paid for at public expense, official, and lists all the candidates for office. This general type may take two forms, however, party column ballot or the office-group ballot. Wyoming uses the party column ballot. Each ballot has a column for each of the political parties with the primary nominees for that party listed under it by office. The party, thus, is the primary feature of this form of ballot. On the office-group ballot, offices, rather than parties, are emphasized with candidates being grouped according to the office that they seek. It should also be mentioned that voting machines are now permissible in Wyoming and three counties use this method of balloting rather than the paper ballot. The voting machine, however, is organized in the same manner as the party column paper ballot in use in the other 20 counties.

When election day is over the results are tallied by the designated election election officials and the candidate for each office that received the largest number of votes is declared the winner, regardless of whether or not he received a majority of the votes cast for that particular office. Usually there are only two candidates and ordinarily one receives a majority, but in some contests such as for legislature in those counties where several seats are up for election, many of those declared elected have not received a majority of votes cast.

INTEREST GROUPS AND POLITICS

The political man can engage in a number of essentially individual acts in the world of politics such as voting, donating money to campaigns, writing letters to the editor, but it is as a member of a social or political group that he achieves his greatest significance in the political world. Single individuals or even small disorganized groups of individuals are unlikely to achieve a great degree of success in influencing the political world unless affiliated with one or more groups. Groups not only influence what an individual wants through the process of political socialization, but attempt to promote the collective interests of their members.

The political process inherent in the making of public policy involves political groups of all sizes, shapes, and purposes. The process is one of conflict, bargaining, compromising, and alliance-making among these groups. Rarely, if ever, is there a clear-cut majority concensus on a particular issue, but rather only a temporary alliance or coalition among the groups involved.

A definition of an interest group is somewhat difficult to formulate because of the complexity of our pluralistic society and the variety of "things" that might sometimes be included in the definition. As used in this context, groups are collectivities or classifications of individuals, organized or unorganized, with similar interests, goals, and attitudes concerning the political system in which they reside. Three points about this definition should be emphasized: (1) primary emphasis in the discussion will center on "organized" groups of various kinds, but "unorganized" segments of the population, for example, consumers, should not be overlooked; (2) the definition is broad enough to include political parties, but for many reasons parties are a special kind of group that is treated separately; (3) only "classifications" relevant to the political system should be considered. This section will be concerned with the various organized interests in Wyoming, and their influence and functions in relation to the Wyoming political system.

Organized Interests in Wyoming

The identification of all interest groups in the state is a difficult and probably unnecessary task. For purposes of suggesting the importance of groups in Wyoming we will be primarily concerned with occupational groups that at times have played a role in the political life of the state.

Agricultural Groups. In Wyoming, an essentially rural state in comparison with most other states, it is not surprising that a few agricultural interest group "giants" have dominated the state political scene for a number of years. These groups have played and probably will continue to play major roles in governmental policy-making at the state level. While they may not always be able to dictate what policy shall be followed, it does seem likely that any one or all of them could "veto" any policy which conflicted significantly with their own. Undoubtedly the two most significant of agriculturally-oriented organizations in Wyoming are the Wyoming Farm Bureau Federation and the Wyoming Stockgrowers Association.

The largest of the agricultural organizations is the Wyoming Farm Bureau Federation. In 1960, 8,751 families in Wyoming were affiliated with this organization.[9] This group is the most highly organized group in the state, having local, county, and state level organizations, and, of course, it is affiliated with the American Farm Bureau Federation which plays a very active role in national affairs. The primary concern of the state and local organizations seems to be the development and use of natural resources and the perceived threat of "encroachment" of the national government on private and local governmental affairs. This is not surprising since the federation has significant numbers of its members in the legislature and among administrators and undoubtedly has more points of access in state and local government than in Washington. Ordinarily, during any session of the legislature the federation sponsors a number of legislative proposals and with the size of the federation delegation in the legislature available, it is usually successful in its legislative program.[10]

Since territorial days the Wyoming Stockgrowers Association has been a very potent and influential organization in state political affairs. During territorial and early statehood days, the stockgrowers were reputed by many to have been one of the most powerful organizations in the country, in some minds comparable to the powerful political machines of the big cities. Until the 1930's very few of the major offices at the state level were held by nonmembers of this group. While its power has waned at various periods of the state's history, in the last 20 years its membership rolls have included two governors, two presidents of the state senate, two speakers of the house, a representative in Congress and two U.S. senators, in addition to significant numbers in the legislature and on administrative boards.

While the stockgrowers suggest that they do not maintain lobbyists in the legislature, some observers maintain that they do not have to since such significant numbers of their membership hold legislative positions, plus the fact that their permanent offices and employees are already stationed in the capital city. On issues the stockgrowers are closely aligned with the Farm Bureau, possibly because many of their members are also involved in Farm Bureau activities. They, like the Farm Bureau, are concerned most about natural resource management and the threat of "bureaucratic meddling" from Washington in local affairs where the association has a firm hold.

Closely related to and allied with the stockgrowers is the Wyoming Woolgrowers Association. In the past these two groups have apparently had vigorous conflicts over use of land and other mutual problems but in recent years they seem to have settled these differences, and their objectives and even their memberships have been closely related. There are many other agricultural organizations which at various times may be important influences on political issues. The Wyoming State Association of Soil and Water Conservation Districts, for example, selects the majority of members to the State Soil and Water

Conservation Committee, in close cooperation with the Farm Bureau. Another closely related interest group is the Wyoming Electrification Association composed of the REA cooperatives in the state, and this organization includes many members of the above organizations. At last count there were at least 16 other organizations in agriculture in the state.

Late in 1962 another organization was brought into being through the combined efforts of the Wyoming Stockgrowers Association and the Wyoming Woolgrowers Association. Concerned primarily with land and related resources, it is called the Western Resources Information Foundation. It is a nonprofit organization purporting to be dedicated to the "orderly private development of lands and resources in the 13 western states."[11] There is no record as yet of the amount of participation by states other than Wyoming. The officers of the organization are taken primarily from the sponsoring organizations although they emphasize that the organization is interested in developing "all" resources and not only livestock interests. This organization has asked for and received considerable technical support and information from the Wyoming agricultural extension service.

Business Groups. Organizations for the promotion of business and related goals are especially numerous, although there is not a great deal of cohesion in their approaches to the affairs of government. In general, the business approach to governmental problems has been conservative with emphasis on reduced governmental spending, low tax rates, and limited governmental intervention in business affairs. In terms of conflict, business most often finds itself in opposition to labor organizations on many matters and, at least in Wyoming politics, on the side of agriculture. In recent years the combination of agriculture and business groups in Wyoming was able to promote the passage of a "right-to-work" law over the objections of labor unions in the state.

There are a number of significant business-oriented groups in Wyoming, including the local and state Chambers of Commerce, Wyoming Retail Merchants Association, and Wyoming Taxpayers Association. In addition there are many specialized groups concerned with particular industries or businesses such as construction, oil and gas, mining, insurance, automobile sales, and tourism. Also, certain specific businesses such as the Union Pacific Railroad in the southern part of the state and the Chicago, Burlington and Quincy in the north at times in the state's history have played important, if not dominant, roles in developing local and state governmental policy.

Besides the "right-to-work" alliance, during recent years various agricultural and business groups have allied themselves in order to present an "over-all stand" with regard to natural and economic resources in the state. This alliance was recently institutionalized in the form of the Wyoming Council for Economic Development which is concerned with developing natural resources and attracting industry into the state. This council is composed of 12 major business and agricultural organizations: Associated General Contractors of Wyoming, Wyoming Water Development Association, Wyoming Automobile Dealers Association, Wyoming Division—Rocky Mountain Oil and Gas Association, Wyoming Farm Bureau Federation, Wyoming Mining Association, Wyoming Oil Industry Committee, Wyoming Retail Merchants Association, Wyoming Chamber of Commerce Executives (advisory), Wyoming Stockgrowers Association, Wyoming Woolgrowers Association, and Wyoming Taxpayers Association (advisory).[12]

Labor Groups. As would be expected in a state that is largely rural and not highly urbanized or industrialized, the labor movement, while not insignificant, has not achieved the high degree of organization or success that it has nationally and in highly industrialized regions of this country. The AFL-CIO is organized in Wyoming along with a number of locals and independent brotherhoods, but their successes at the state level have been somewhat limited. Union management fought vigorously, but in vain, against the right-to-work proposal in 1963. Using this as a 1964 campaign slogan, labor was probably more highly organized than at any other time in the history of the state and undoubtedly played a major role in the Democratic sweep in Wyoming in 1964. Since then they have been, however, unable to secure repeal of right-to-work against the combined interests of business and agriculture.

Professional Groups. Although relatively small in terms of total numbers in the society, professional groups have had, and undoubtedly will continue to have, significant influence in the political system. This influence presumably is related to the relatively high degree of status and prestige that is associated with professional achievements and training.

In Wyoming the usual professional groups exist and enter into the political arena when their particular interests are involved. The Wyoming Bar Association, for example, often is concerned with the nature of the legal structure and procedure practiced in the state. The Wyoming Medical Association is concerned with matters of health and medicine, and the Wyoming Engineering Society is concerned about standards of professional competence and awarding of contracts by the state. In recent years the Wyoming Education Association has begun to flex its political muscles on behalf of Wyoming teachers. A comprehensive list of other such organizations is not possible nor would it be entirely fruitful in this work.

Some emphasis should also be given here to "professionals" within the governmental structure—state governmental employees. One might even make a case for maintaining that the bureaucracy is a special occupational grouping deserving separate occupational categorization. With the emergence of a technological society, government also has become more and more specialized, employing increasing numbers of specialists and technicians. Since these personnel are within the governmental decision-making centers they are in extremely good positions to influence the whole decision-making process by supplying information, making recommendations, and implementing or not implementing over-all political programs.

In a recent survey Wyoming administrators indicated that as a group they were very active in their respective professions.[13] Of the administrators surveyed, 80 per cent indicated that they belonged to one or more professional organizations. The most sizeable membership in any one group was that in the Wyoming Engineering Society and this organization has taken relatively vigorous stands on a number of state governmental issues, including primarily water and resource-related issues. At the state level there are at least three agricultural extension associations—Wyoming County Agricultural Agents Association, Wyoming Home Demonstration Agents Association, and the Agricultural Extension Service Specialists Association—which on occasion have adopted resolutions pertaining to agricultural programs. There are also countless professional organizations related to maintenance and preservation of wildlife and fish to which a number of game and fish personnel belong. It seems that many of the health and game and fish agencies have affiliated to a greater extent with national level professional organizations related to their specialty than to local or state level organizations of similar types. Because of these associations and memberships, therefore, it is important that the "bureaucracy" be assigned a place of importance in the determination and execution of state governmental policy.

Other Interest Groups. In any state and in the nation as a whole there are a variety of other interests that at times are seemingly influential in the governmental process. Many of these are single-issue groups and therefore are not vitally concerned with the broad range of governmental policy. In Wyoming, for Example, "conservation" has become a significant issue and great numbers of organizations have sprung up around it. These groups, however, while they are often at odds with agricultural and business groups in the state, have not made many inroads into state governmental policy-making. The conservation movement appears to be a national movement and these types of groups appear to perceive their best opportunities at the national level of government. While such groups exist at the state level in Wyoming, and they have loosely federated into the Wyoming Conservation Association, they have not taken many major stands on state issues. On national issues the Wyoming groups have allied themselves with such conservation giants as the Izaak Walton League, the Wilderness Society, the National Wildlife Federation, and the National Parks Association.

Veterans, through the American Legion and the Veterans of Foreign Wars, have had considerable influence at the state and national levels on various issues such as homestead and tax exemptions, pensions, hospitalization, and bonuses. The League of Women Voters has made many studies of state and local government and at times has had an impact. Often religious and ethnic groups have been influential although Wyoming has a relatively homogeneous population and ethnic or religious issues have been at a minimum.

These nonoccupational groups in society do seem to have one significant effect on the political game. They provide what has been called "crisscross" of interests in that most such groups include many different occupations in their memberships, thus tending to modify the intensity of the occupational group struggle through multiple and cross-memberships.

Interest Groups and Political Influence

Extragovernmental Influence. Interest groups use a variety of techniques and methods for influencing political affairs, most of which might be classed as "propaganda" or in a more acceptable term, "public relations." Modern methods of communication such as radio, newspapers, television allow interest groups many avenues of approach to influencing both the general public and governmental officials. Public relations activities by interest groups are designed to create the illusion of acceptability and respectability. If this atmosphere of approval can be created and maintained through advertising and sponsorship of worthwhile projects, specific political programs of the interest group will probably also tend to be somewhat more acceptable. Many so-called advertising campaigns thus are designed not so much to sell a particular product but to sell the company, for example, the large-scale advertising of "investor-owned utilities." Sponsorship of scholarships, movies, little league baseball teams, Boy Scout troops, and other similar projects receive favorable publicity and attempt to equate particular group interests with the "general interest."

Interest groups also participate in a number of activities designed to put into political office those individuals who are most sympathetic with group goals and objectives. Groups, in some cases, not only actively support and campaign for particular individuals, but donate money and human resources to the political parties so that this objective will be accomplished. While business has been particularly successful in public relations activities because of its vast financial resources, agriculture and labor have been more successful through their electioneering activities.

Intra-governmental Activities. The problem of access to strategic points of governmental decision-making is, of course, the heart of group activity in the political system. While most groups involved in the political process are apparently not capable of determining exactly what governmental policy at any particular level of government will be, they seek to influence this policy to the greatest extent possible. In other words, while most groups are not able to dictate policy, they seek to obtain policies which are least objectionable to them or at least to "veto" those policies which conflict with their own basic objectives.

Differential advantages, or access points, in state government, which various groups seek to obtain and maintain, affect the output of the political system considerably. Certain interests and groups are directly connected to specific governmental units, both formally and informally. This arrangement means that these interests and groups are guaranteed a degree of status that others do not have. It also suggests that more favorable policy considerations now and in the future will be made to these groups.

Access to the political structure is most clearly evident in the legislative branch through the use of lobbying. The lobbyist has a great many points in the complex legislative system at which he can hope to exert influence or use his "veto" power, but lobbying not only includes the actual pressuring of legislators but providing them with information and materials and reminding them of their own backgrounds, whether agricultural or business, when crucial issues come before the legislature. Because of the short legislative session and lack of legislative staff in Wyoming and most other states, lobbyists are often responsible for drafting bills, providing material and information for debate and discussion, whether the specific bill at issue is of direct concern to the lobbyist or not.

Of even greater importance than lobbying in the legislature, however, is the day-to-day influence of interest groups in the administrative branch of government. Both formally and informally interest groups have a close working relationship with the many administrative offices and bureaus in state and national government. Agricultural groups in Wyoming, for example, are tied directly to several agencies by various means. Legally the composition of the state board of agriculture and state soil and water conservation committee must be made up of individuals employed in agriculture. Informally, many members of other boards and commissions such as the game and fish commission and the natural resource board have historically been drawn primarily from agricultural and related occupations. Also, occupational licensing boards' memberships generally are exclusively drawn from the interest groups being regulated such as the bar association, real estate association, cosmetologists, dentists, and other similar occupations. These agencies thus are linked rather closely to specific interest groups and have developed much the same outlook as the groups espouse.

The differential advantages and representation of certain groups and interests in Wyoming seems to have precipitated or at least encouraged the multiplicity of agencies in state government; it tends to create conflict situations among agencies; and, it suggests that attempts to reorganize state government would be in for considerable trouble.

Functions of Interest Groups. This general discussion of the role of interest groups in Wyoming might be summed up by emphasizing the usefulness of groups in the political system. (1) Groups serve as educational agencies in the sense that they often campaign widely on behalf of their programs and even candidates. In this process the general citizenry, legislators, and administrators are made aware of some of the crucial issues facing state and nation. (2) Groups serve in a representative capacity which tends to supplement the formal areal and political representation in the legislature and other elective offices. (3) Groups provide access to the political decision-making centers for their membership that would not be available to the individual citizen. (4) Closely related to the last point, groups perform an integrating function in linking individuals to the decision-making centers and making legitimate the decisions made by those centers.

FOOTNOTES

1. Robert F. Karsch, *The Government of Missouri*, 8th edition, Columbia: Lucas Brothers Publishers, 1963, pages 25, 33, 34.
2. *Wyoming Statutes*, 1957, 22-118. 3.
3. Taken largely from the definition of political parties by Austin Ranney and Wilmoore Kendall, *Democracy and the American Party System*, New York: Harcourt, Brace & World, Inc., 1956.
4. See generally *Wyoming Statutes*, 1957, 22-118. 5 through 22-118. 9 for legal organizational requirements of political parties in Wyoming.
5. *Ibid.*, 22-118. 28.
6. *Wyoming Constitution*, Art. VI, Sec. 2; *Wyoming Statutes*, 1957, 22-118. 3.
7. *Ibid.*
8. *Ibid.*, 22-153 to 22-177.
9. American Farm Bureau Federation, *Official News Letter*, Vol. 39, No. 34, May 22, 1960, page 133.
10. See John B. Richard, *State Administration and Water Resources in Wyoming*, (unpublished Ph.D. dissertation, University of Illinois, 1965).
11. *The Wyoming Stockman-Farmer*, Cheyenne, Wyoming, December, 1962, page 26.
12. *Ibid.*, June, 1963, page 16.
13. Richard, *op. cit.*, pages 132, 146.

CHAPTER THREE

The State Legislature, Politics and Legislation

The heart of state government is the state legislature. The primary function of a legislative body is to establish the basic rules of order for a political system, whether state or nation. This includes the determination of general governmental policy as to services that are to be provided and the nature of the governmental structure that will provide them. In other words, it is the legislature which establishes the basic legal pattern and framework within which citizens and governmental agencies operate. Although at times the legislature may only legitimize decisions which have been made elsewhere, it is ultimately responsible for the final policy decision.

LEGISLATIVE POWERS AND LIMITATIONS

In a federal system governmental powers, in a legal sense, are divided between a central government and territorial governments (states), each having some functions to perform. According to this constitutional distribution of powers, the national government has those powers delegated to it by the Constitution and those which can be reasonably implied from the enumerated constitutional powers, and the states have all those powers not delegated to the national government and not expressly denied by the Constitution. Some of these reserved powers of the state are delegated by the state constitution to the executive and judicial branches of state government, but all the remaining powers of government belong to the state legislature, limited only by such specific limitations as may be contained in the state constitution. It is to these "residual" powers of the legislature, along with some state constitutional limitations, to which we now turn.

Powers and Functions of the Legislature

Lawmaking. The most important power of a legislature is its general lawmaking or legislative power. The residual character of the powers of the state legislature, as just described, seems to suggest that the state legislature's lawmaking power is extremely broad and, while limited by some state and national constitutional provisions, extends to nearly any area of public concern. Included in this residuum of state legislative power is what is often called the "police power." In general terms this may be defined as the power to provide for the health, safety, morals, and welfare of the people of the state. The national Congress has no such general power, and the state, therefore, is responsible ultimately for determining the "public interest," however that may be defined.

Though it would be impossible to list all the specific legislative prerogatives which might be included under this broad scope of power, or to predict future powers to be exercised under its guise, the following examples will serve to at least suggest the breadth of state legislative powers: taxation and expenditure of public funds (power of the purse); regulation of marriage and divorce; provision for education and educational institutions; definition of crimes and their punishment; administration of state institutions; regulation of labor and conditions of work; maintenance of the National Guard; protection of fish and wildlife; licensing of professions such as medicine, teaching, veterinary medicine, barbering, plumbing, and dentistry; incorporation of businesses and banking; regulation of public utilities. Thus, the general lawmaking power of the legislature extends to an extremely broad, though not limitless, range of activities.

Executive and Administrative Powers. The legislature not only has general lawmaking powers but also a number of essentially non-lawmaking powers. The state senate exercises a primarily executive power when it participates in the appointment of state executive officers. Many state officials are appointed by the governor "with the advice and consent of the state senate." Further, just as the United States Senate must give its advice and consent to international treaties entered into by the United States, the state legislature performs an executive function in approving or disapproving interstate compacts "negotiated" by the state executive.

The state legislature also plays an administrative role in the sense that it creates the nonconstitutional agencies in the executive branch of government. While state legislatures largely refrain from directly supervising state executive agencies, they do have a supervisory and directory responsibility with regard to the execution of general policies by state executive agencies. Finally, the legislature is responsible for the creation and supervision of local units of government, including counties, municipalities, and special districts.

Judicial Powers. The judicial power of the legislature is most clearly shown in its power to impeach and remove executive and judicial officers of the state. The state constitution specifies that the "power of impeachment shall vest in the house of representatives; the concurrence of a majority of all members being necessary to the exercise thereof."[1] Impeachment charges are tried by the senate with a two-thirds majority of all senators required for conviction. The governor and "any other state and judicial officers except justices of the peace," are liable to impeachment for "high crimes and misdemeanors, or malfeasance in office."[2] Penalty for conviction is removal from office and disqualification for further office-holding, although the impeached individual might subsequently be prosecuted in a regular court proceeding.

The judicial power of the legislature is also illustrated by its powers relative to the judicial branch of government. Establishment of municipal courts, rules and regulations concerning relationships of inferior courts to the supreme court, terms of the supreme court and district courts, salaries of judges, judicial districts, and election of justices of the peace, are delineated by the constitution as subject to the discretion of the legislature.[3]

Electoral Power. Although it is sometimes included in the general lawmaking powers of the legislature, the electoral function seems to be in a category by itself. This power or function is two-fold: (1) the legislature is responsible for setting the time, manner, and place for election of state and local officials[4]; and, (2) each house of the legislature is the judge of the election returns and qualifications of its own members.[5]

Constituent Powers. As described in an earlier chapter the state legislature has a role to play in the amending of the state constitution. This is its constituent power. Amendments to the state constitution may be proposed in either house of the legislature and if two-thirds of the members of each house approve, the proposed amendment is submitted to the electorate for ratification.[6] Also, the legislature, by two-thirds vote of the members of each house, may submit to the electorate a proposal for calling a constitutional convention, and if ratified by a majority of the electors participating in the election, the legislature at the next session provides for calling the convention.[7] Finally, the state legislature may participate in the ratification of amendments to the national Constitution when such proposals are submitted to it.

Investigatory Powers. Although usually not expressly granted by a constitution, legislative bodies ordinarily are considered to have general investigatory powers. Investigations by the legislature may center on a number of topics including the operation of a particular department or agency such as the highway department, alleged fraud in elections, needs of education, or similar problems. The Wyoming legislature, at times in the past, has provided for an interim legislative committee and a legislative council, charging these agencies to investigate certain areas of concern. The purpose of an investigation is presumably to furnish the informational basis for any subsequent legislation on a particular topic.

Limitations on State Legislative Powers

Though the residual powers of the state legislature are far-reaching, there are some limitations imposed on those powers. The two primary sources of restrictions on legislative powers are the national Constitution and the state constitution.

National Constitutional Limitations. The primary national restrictions on state powers are contained in Article I, Section 10, and Amendments XIII, XIV, IV, XIX, XXIV. For example, states may not pass bills of attainder or ex post facto laws; enter into treaties; coin money or issue currency; grant titles of nobility; impair contracts; permit slavery; abridge privileges and immunities of citizens of the United States; deny equal protection of the laws; deprive any person of "life, liberty, or property without due process of law"; or impose a poll tax. Further, the due process clause of the Fourteenth Amendment has been interpreted by the national courts to preclude states from interference with the First Amendment freedoms such as press, speech, religion, assembly, and petition.

State Constitutional Limitations. A state constitution normally is excessively verbose and as a result usually includes several restrictions on legislative power. Generally, these restrictions include: (1) fiscal limitations; (2) a bill of rights; (3) prohibitions on special legislation and delegation of powers by the legislature.

The Wyoming constitution contains several restrictions on the fiscal power of the legislature reflecting the general 19th century distrust of legislative power. A few illustrations of these financial limitations are: state, county, and city property tax levy limits; certain exemptions from taxation; state school property tax limits; limits on disposition of gasoline and road taxes; state, county, and city debt limits; and, limits on "internal improvements" expenditures unless authorized by two-thirds vote of the people.[8] The limitation on works of improvement, however, has been modified considerably so as not to include highway construction, water works and irrigation works, and construction, maintenance, or improvement of public airports and facilities.[9]

The state legislature is also limited regarding certain civil rights of the citizenry. The Declaration of Rights of the state constitution contains 37 sections, many of which might be considered limitations on legislative powers. The initiative and referendum approved by the voters in 1968 could possibly limit the legislature.

Finally, the state constitution prohibits the legislature from passing special legislation and prohibits delegation of power by the legislature. The constitution includes a lengthy list of situations in which special or local legislation might be a temptation and prohibits the legislature from doing such when a law of general application would suffice.[10] The constitution also specifically forbids the legislature to delegate its power to perform legislative functions to any other department of government or nongovernmental agency or association.[11]

APPORTIONMENT AND REPRESENTATION

Apportionment is a complex problem to which any legislative body must necessarily periodically turn its attention. Seats in the legislature must be allocated or assigned to specific constituencies in the state or in the nation depending upon which legislative body is concerned. There are not any absolute "principles" which are inherently "correct" or "true" or which have more merit necessarily than any other plans or proposals that may be put forward. It is a problem, however, that must be solved. The Supreme Court of the United States has made it absolutely clear that periodic reapportionment must be accomplished by the states in both houses of the state legislature. This criterion resulted from the decision made in the landmark case of *Baker* vs. *Carr* in 1962.[12]

The significance of the *Baker* case was that for the first time the Supreme Court indicated that such a case was justiciable. Prior to this decision the court had indicated in a number of other decisions that such suits involved "political questions," and that the court lacked jurisdiction in such matters. Thus the court indicated that citizens could seek a judicial remedy if they felt that apportionment of a legislative body involved "invidious discrimination" and deprived them of their right to "equal protection of the laws" under the Fourteenth Amendment to the national Constitution. The *Baker* case, however, did not immediately answer a number of significant questions concerning apportionment. Did this ruling of "one man, one vote" apply to both houses of a state legislature? What constituted "invidious discrimination"? Did the ruling also apply to congressional districts?

In two other decisions the United States Supreme Court seemed to answer these major questions raised by the *Baker* case. In *Wesberry* vs. *Sanders*,[13] the court indicated that congressional districts must be based on the "one man, one vote" principle and be of relatively equal size. In July, 1964, the court finally reached a decision in the much thornier problem of determining the nature of state legislative apportionment schemes. In *Reynolds* vs. *Sims*,[14] the court directed that both houses of state legislatures must be based on population and that so-called "little Federal Plans" were not permissible. Many states, including Wyoming, had based representation in the legislature on the scheme used in the national Constitution—that is, one house is based on population and one is based on equal representation of states regardless of size. The argument used by the court was essentially that counties were not sovereign units in a federal system in the same sense that states were united in the federal government. Counties, the court said, were related to the state government in a unitary system in which they did not retain individual autonomy or sovereignty.

As a result of the *Baker* decision, Wyoming and almost all the other states were faced with the problem of reapportioning the state legislature. Prior to this decision, Wyoming's bicameral legislature contained 27 senators and 56 representatives. The state constitution required that legislative apportionment was to be based "as nearly as may be" on population, except that each county was to constitute a legislative district and must have at least one senator and one representative. Further constitutional limitation determined the relative sizes of the two houses in that the number of members of the house was not to be less than twice nor greater than three times the number of members in the senate.[15] Because of the great population discrepancies among the 23 counties, the apportionment of the legislature did not meet the "one man, one vote" requirement of the court.

The legislature, prior to 1963, had last reapportioned its membership in 1933, and there is little doubt that many rural areas were grossly over-represented in the legislature. The population per representative ranged from a low of 2,930 to a high of 10,025 in the house of representatives and 3,062 to 30,075 in the state senate. In the house the average population deviation per representative was 2,212, or 37.5 per cent of the average population per representative. In the senate the discrepancy among districts was even greater, resulting in an average population deviation per representative of 8,216, or 55.4 per cent of the average population per senator.

Probably as a result of the *Baker* case and a suit in a state court by a citizens' group, the 1963 legislature passed the first reapportionment bill in 30 years. Although this apportionment was immediately challenged in the federal courts, it provided a reasonably close approximation to population for each representative in the house. In the new house there were still some discrepancies because of constitutional restrictions, but the average deviation in the districts as a whole was only 463 persons per district, or 8.5 per cent of the average population per representative. In the senate, however, the average deviation was 7,531, or 57.0 per cent of the average population per senator. A group of citizens immediately challenged the constitutionality of this apportionment in both houses, but particularly in the senate.

In January, 1964, a three-judge federal court heard the case of *Schaefer* vs. *Thomson*[16] in which the constitutionality of the 1963 legislative apportionment act was questioned. The court, however, pending the decision of the United States Supreme Court on "little Federal Plans," reserved decision until the Supreme Court acted. When the *Reynolds* decision was made it was evident what the decision in Wyoming's case would be. The governor immediately called the state legislature into special session in July, 1964, in an attempt to solve the problem but no action was forthcoming amid charges and countercharges. In November, 1964, the three-judge federal court made its decision, indicating that the lower house was properly apportioned, but that the state senate must be apportioned according to population. If this reapportionment, the court indicated, was not accomplished by the 1965 session of the legislature, it would reapportion the legislature itself. The court further ordered the legislature to disregard the limiting provisions of the state constitution in arriving at a "fair" apportionment.

Even though it was under a direct order of the federal court, the 1965 legislature did not take any action on apportionment. With a divided legislature, the house controlled by Democrats and the senate by Republicans, no plan could be formulated acceptable to both parties. The governor made a strong plea for action on this problem in his message to the legislature and submitted a detailed plan for apportionment. Five other bills were introduced on this topic. One, a bill sponsored by the house Democrats, did pass the house, but none of the propsals was acceptable to both houses, both parties, and urban and rural interests.

As a result of the failure of the legislature to act, the federal court on October 7, 1965, ordered a reapportionment of the Wyoming state senate. The court increased the size of the senate from 25 to 30 members and created 17 senatorial districts out of the 23 counties in the state. Laramie county received five senators; Natrona, four; Fremont and Hot Springs, three; Albany, Sheridan, Park, and Sweetwater, two each; and one senator each to the other districts some of which are single counties, some combinations of counties, and one divided county. The smallest senatorial district created was Platte county with 7,195 people and the largest was Carbon with 14,937 people. All senators, as well as representatives, are elected at large from each county or district and all senators, regardless of whether or not their terms had expired, would have to seek election in the 1966 election. Mathematically, this decision meant that 47 per cent of the population could elect a majority (53.3 per cent) of the senate.

Current apportionment of the Wyoming Senate is shown in Table 7. The House apportionment is shown in Table 8. In addition, these two tables indicate the sizes of average districts, largest districts, smallest districts, and ratios of largest to smallest districts.

Although the court has decreed a legislative apportionment scheme, the problem is not automatically solved. Apportionment is a perennial problem. Changes in population, migration, and a multitude of factors will create new demands for change. Any system that may be devised will distribute advantages and disadvantages to some people and not to others. No system of representation can possibly do perfect justice to every voter and to every interest in the state. Even the court plan is already under attack in some circles.

At-large elections and the use of the "plurality principle" of certifying as elected the candidates receiving the greatest number of votes in an area, even though the number of votes cast for each is considerably smaller than the combined votes for the losing candidates, it is alleged, often leaves a majority of voters without representatives of their choosing. It is possible that a minority interest or ethnic group has never had a representative, or never will, of its own choosing and who can represent their interests in the legislature. In other words, at-large elections often mean that one party wins all the seats in a multi-member district and the minority is not represented in proportion to its strength. At-large elections also lengthen the ballot considerably. Laramie county voters, for example, has to choose 11 representatives and five senators along with decisions

TABLE 7
Wyoming Senate
Apportionment 1974

Senate District	No. of Seats	Population
Albany	2	26,431
Big Horn	1	10,202
Campbell-Johnson	2	18,544
Carbon	1	13,354
Converse-Niobrara	1	8,862
Crook-Weston	1	10,842
Fremont	2	28,352
Goshen-Platte	2	17,371
Hot Springs-Washakie	1	12,521
Laramie	5	56,360
Uinta-So. Lincoln	1	11,420
Natrona	4	51,264
Park	2	17,752
Sheridan	2	17,852
Sublette-Teton-No. Lincoln	1	12,898
Sweetwater	2	18,391
	30	332,416

Largest District: Fremont, 14,176 people per senator. Smallest District: Platte-Goshen, 8,685 people per senator. Average District: 11,080 people per senator. Ratio of Largest to Smallest District: 1.6:1.

TABLE 8
Wyoming House of Representatives
Apportionment 1974

House District	No. of Seats	Population
Albany	5	26,431
Big Horn	2	10,202
Campbell	2	12,957
Carbon	3	13,354
Converse	1	5,938
Crook	1	4,535
Fremont	5	28,352
Goshen	2	10,885
Hot Springs	1	4,952
Johnson	1	5,587
Laramie	11	56,360
Lincoln	2	8,640
Natrona	10	51,264
Niobrara	1	2,924
Park	3	17,752
Platte	1	6,486
Sheridan	3	17,852
Sublette	1	3,755
Sweetwater	3	18,391
Teton	1	4,823
Uinta	1	7,100
Washakie	1	7,569
Weston	1	6,307
	62	332,416

Largest District: Washakie, 7,569 people per representative. Smallest District: Niobrara, 2,924 people per representative. Average District: 5,361 people per representative. Ratio of Largest to Smallest District: 2.6:1.

concerning other executive officials and substantive issues. The ordinary voter, it is alleged, is in no position to make an informed and intelligent judgement on so many candidates and issues.

SOCIAL BACKGROUNDS OF WYOMING LEGISLATORS[17]

Who are Wyoming's legislators? Do they represent a cross section of the state's population? How well prepared is the typical legislator, and from what groups in society is he recruited? How did the reapportionment ordered by the federal court affect the composition of the Wyoming legislature? Although our answers to these questions are based on limited data, some general observations might be made about the types of persons who are likely to be found in the Wyoming legislature.

The legal prerequisites for election to the Wyoming legislature are minimal. Senators need only be 25; representatives, 21 years of age. In either house, legislators must be citizens of the United States and of Wyoming, and must have resided in the state for one year prior to their election.[18]

Wyoming legislators do not represent a cross section of the Wyoming citizenry. In terms of occupation and education, an average legislator differs a great deal from the average Wyoming citizen. In Table 9 it can be seen that the largest occupational group in the House and the second largest group in the Senate during the period of 1965-1973 were employed in professional fields. Only 14.5 per cent of Wyoming's work force were employed in professional occupations. Actually the legislators who were professionals were primarily lawyers and this is not the case among professionals in the state's work force. In agriculture it can be seen that there has been a decline in representation over the period indicated which does reflect the smaller number of citizens who are involved in agricultural occupations. It probably also represents the reapportionment which has occurred. There is not a completely satisfactory explanation why some occupations are overrepresented although some tentative answers might be mentioned. Professionals perhaps have more opportunity to take time off to attend legislative sessions than do blue collar workers. Lawyers usually are professional representors and a legislative job fits into this category. As a matter-of-fact the legal profession is usually a logical starting point for an aspiring politician.

In terms of formal education and training again we find that the legislators are more highly educated than the average population of the state. In 1970 the Census Bureau reported that approximately 12 per cent of the adult population over 25 had college degrees. The comparable figure for Wyoming legislators during the five terms shown in Table 10 was 61 per cent for the House and 56 per cent for the Senate.

In Tables 11 and 12 religious preferences and organizational memberships are shown. In terms of religious preference the Wyoming legislators do show a

TABLE 9
Occupations of Wyoming Legislators—1965-1973 (in per cent)

	1965		1967		1969		1971		1973	
	House	Senate	House	Senate	House	Senate	House	Senate	House	Senate
Agriculture*	26.2	40.0	23.0	23.3	21.3	23.3	24.6	26.7	22.6	26.7
Business	27.9	28.0	32.9	40.0	34.5	50.0	24.6	36.7	32.3	43.3
Professional										
Lawyers	19.7	8.0	19.7	23.3	18.0	20.0	9.8	23.3	17.7	20.0
Other Professional	19.7	20.0	16.4	13.4	19.7	6.7	24.6	13.3	19.4	6.7
Total Professional	39.4	28.0	36.0	36.7	37.7	26.7	34.4	36.6	37.1	26.7
Other Occupations	6.5	4.0	8.1	0.0	6.5	0.0	16.4	0.0	8.0	3.3
Total	100.0	100.0	100.0	100.0	100.0	100.0	100.0	100.0	100.0	100.0
	N = (61)	N = (25)	N = (61)	N = (30)	N = (61)	N = (30)	N = (61)	N = (30)	N = (61)	N = (30)

Source: B. Oliver Walter and Kendall Baker, *The Wyoming Legislature: Lawmakers, The Public and the Press*, Laramie: Government Research Bureau, University of Wyoming, 1973, pp. 5-6.

TABLE 10
Formal Education of Wyoming Legislators—1965-1973 (in per cent)

	1965		1967		1969		1971		1973	
	House	Senate	House	Senate	House	Senate	House	Senate	House	Senate
High School	16.4	24.0	19.8	13.3	11.5	13.3	14.8	13.3	14.5	10.0
Some College	18.0	20.0	21.3	16.7	18.0	16.7	19.7	23.3	14.4	16.7
College Degree	29.4	20.0	21.3	23.3	32.8	23.3	31.1	26.7	30.7	40.0
Post Graduate Degree	6.6	8.0	13.0	6.7	11.5	3.3	16.4	3.3	14.5	3.3
Professional Degree	23.0	20.0	21.3	26.7	21.3	30.0	13.1	23.3	21.0	20.0
Trade or Business School	6.6	16.0	3.3	13.4	16.4	10.0	18.0	3.3	4.8	3.3
No Answer	0.0	0.0	0.0	0.0	0.0	0.0	3.3	0.0	0.0	0.0
Total	100.0	100.0	100.0	100.0	100.0	100.0	100.0	100.0	100.0	100.0
	N = (61)	N = (25)	N = (61)	N = (30)	N = (61)	N = (30)	N = (61)	N = (30)	N = (62)	N = (30)

Source: B. Oliver Walter and Kendall Baker, *The Wyoming Legislature: Lawmakers, The Public and the Press*, Laramie: Government Research Bureau, University of Wyoming, 1973, pp. 11-12.

remarkable similarity to the Wyoming population. In terms of membership in organizations, legislators are clearly more gregarious and belong to far more organizations than do ordinary citizens.

TABLE 11
Religious Preference of 1971 and 1973
Wyoming Legislators (in per cent)

	House		Senate	
	1971	1973	1971	1973
Catholic	24.6	22.6	23.7	26.6
Episcopal	13.1	16.0	23.3	16.7
Methodist	14.8	14.5	16.7	13.3
Congregational	3.3	3.2	6.7	6.7
Presbyterian	8.2	19.4	3.3	6.7
Lutheran	5.0	6.5	6.7	3.3
Baptist	5.1	0.0	6.7	6.7
Protestant (no specific denomination mentioned)	8.2	8.1	10.0	13.3
Morman	6.6	3.2	3.3	6.7
No Answer	13.1	6.5		0.0
Total	100.0	100.0	100.0	100.0
	N = (61)	N = (62)	N = (30)	N = (30)

Source: B. Oliver Walter and Kendall Baker, *The Wyoming Legislature: Lawmakers, The Public and the Press,* Laramie: Government Research Bureau, University of Wyoming, 1973.

TABLE 12
Organizational Membership of 1971 and 1973
Wyoming Legislators

	House		Senate	
	1971	1973	1971	1973
Bar Association	9.8	17.7	16.6	16.6
Stockgrowers	19.7	12.9	23.3	26.7
Farm Bureau	23.0	14.5	30.0	26.7
Chamber of Commerce or Jaycees	34.4	35.5	33.3	36.7
Social Organizations	70.5	72.6	70.0	70.0
American Legion or VFW	31.4	35.5	36.7	36.7
Average number of group memberships excluding religion	4.0	4.5	4.6	4.7

Source: B Oliver Walter and Kendall Baker, *The Wyoming Legislature: Lawmakers, The Public and the Press,* Laramie: Government Research Bureau, University of Wyoming, 1973.

To what extent has reapportionment been responsible for the changes noted in the preceding paragraphs? It would appear that reapportionment has been a substantial force in these changes, though it was by no means the sole factor. As we have seen, the electoral forces at work in the 1964 election had a profound effect on the Wyoming legislature. That election, which was a devastating event in that the Republican Party was reduced to far below its normal strength, effected two notable changes on the state legislature: a trend of lessening farmer-rancher representation was started, and the educational level of the legislature was drastically reduced. Reapportionment, it seems, has reinforced the trend of less agricultural representation. The counties which gained the most from reapportionment—namely Laramie, Natrona, and Fremont counties—have been most likely to send professional men to the legislature and least likely to elect farmers and ranchers. However, the lowering of educational level wrought by the 1964 election has been sharply reversed in the reapportioned legislatures since 1965. Again, the increase of attorneys, educators, and other professional men seems to have played the major role.

The most apparent difference since the court-ordered reapportionment has been the infusion of fresh personnel into both houses of legislature. Of the 86 lawmakers who comprised the last self-apportioned legislature in 1965, only 42 remained when the 1969 legislature convened. When, in 1965, the federal court combined 12 counties into six senatorial districts, the inevitable result was the loss of incumbent senators. Six of the "re-districted senators" having an aggregated total of 98 years' service in the Wyoming legislature decided not to stand for re-election. Three more having 32 years' total tenure were defeated in clashes with other incumbent senators. In addition to the senators whose seats were re-districted out of existence, there arrived in Cheyenne new senators from newly-created seats from Laramie, Natrona, Fremont, Albany, and Park counties. These counties had been awarded more Senate seats by the federal court. In the first legislative session after the court-ordered reapportionment, 18 of the 30 senators were freshmen. As the 1969 legislature convened, the average length of service for the 30 senators was four years in that body, and 7.3 years service in both houses of the legislature. The comparable figures for the 1963 Senate were 5.4 years in the Senate and 9.5 years experience in both houses.

In sum, then, we can say that: (1) Wyoming's legislators are an elite with a much higher educational level and higher level of civic participation than the average citizen; (2) Farmer and rancher membership in the Wyoming legislature has declined dramatically in the decade of the 60's, but the agricultural occupations are still over-represented in terms of relative population; (3) Professional and business men are increasing their numbers in the legislature and this has led to an increase in the educational level of the lawmaking body; (4) The typical legislator has had a substantial amount of previous experience either in the legislature or in local government, and (5) Reapportionment, in accordance with the U.S. Supreme Court's "one-man, one-vote" doctrine, seems to have contributed to various changes in the Wyoming legislature the most apparent of which is the recruitment of new personnel to replace veteran legislators.

Finally, it might be said that, due to the relatively high educational level of Wyoming's legislators and due to the complete exclusion of blue-collar workers from the lawmaking body, the Wyoming Legislature does not constitute an accurate cross section of the state's people. However, the inclination of voters to select legislators of higher education than they and from higher occupational strata than they is really not unusual. To the contrary, it seems to be one of the identifying features of representative democracy in the United States.

LEGISLATIVE STRUCTURE AND ORGANIZATION

Organization of the Wyoming legislature is similar to that which is found in the national Congress. Although the state senate is actually a continuing body because of staggered terms of its members, both houses must select their officers every two years and determine the division of work by choosing committee chairmen and members. The whole process of legislative organization is under the general direction of the two political parties. In this section we shall look at the party framework in the legislature, the officers and leaders of the legislature, and the committee system.

The Partisan Framework in the Legislature

Despite some degree of divided control of state government between Democrats and Republicans during approximately 40 per cent of the entire period of the state's history, "partisanship," in the sense of relatively cohesive and disciplined parties, appears to be somewhat limited within the legislature and in the relationships between the governor and the legislature.

A party vote is one on which a majority of one party votes against the majority of the other party. Although it varies, as can be seen from Table 13, the percentage of party votes was not over 50 percent in either the House or the Senate for the 1965, 1967, 1969 or 1973 sessions. (Unfortunately, we do not have data for the 1971 session.)

TABLE 13
Party Votes in Wyoming Legislature (1965-1973)

	House	No. of Votes	Senate	No. of Votes
1965	46.5%	86	23.3%	43
1967	38.0%	79	30.4%	102
1969	16.7%	84	17.8%	90
1973	31.8%	130	40.0%	130

Source: B. Oliver Walter and Kendall Baker, *The Wyoming Legislature: Lawmakers, The Public and the Press,* Laramie: GRB, 1973, p. 28.

When we compare Wyoming to other state legislatures we find little difference between the Equality state and her neighbors. On only about a third of the controversial legislative votes does the majority of one party vote against the majority of the other in any of these states.

There are a number of reasons why strong two-party politics do not dominate legislative policy-making in Wyoming. The generally homogeneous character of the population, alluded to in an earlier chapter, probably plays an important role. There is not a clear-cut division of parties along urban-rural or industrial-agricultural lines. In many states the large urban areas with highly developed industrial complexes provide the basis for Democratic strength, while the suburbs and rural areas support largely Republican legislators. In Wyoming, while there is something of an urban-rural split between north and south, it is not so clear cut. Rather, it would seem that there is a three-way split among the larger cities, the smaller towns, and the rural areas, all of which make homogeneous legislative parties with strong platforms and similar constituencies difficult to attain. In Wyoming then, Democrats do not necessarily represent only the larger cities and Republicans the rural or suburban areas, with each legislative party member responding to a similar type of constituency. Pressure group or constituency voting is thus more likely to be important, if not actually replace cohesive party voting, in the absence of strong legislative political parties.[19]

Presiding Officers. There is one legislative topic in which the political party organization in the legislature plays a prominent role—choosing the leadership. The parties in each house, in caucuses prior to the opening of the biennial session, choose one of the members, a senior member, to be a candidate for the position of speaker of the house or president of the senate. In one of the few times when strict party voting is the rule, the majority party candidate is elected although often there is a formal unanimous vote by all members endorsing the candidate of the majority party.

In Wyoming, in contrast with most other states and Congress, the presiding officers of both houses are chosen by the respective memberships of the two houses. In most states the presiding officer of the senate is the lieutenant governor, just as the vice-president of the United States is president of the United States Senate. In Wyoming, however, there is no office of lieutenant governor and the senate chooses a president from its membership. The house, as in all other states and the national Congress, chooses from its membership a speaker of the house. For the first time in history in 1969, the speaker is a woman.

Both the speaker and the president have similar duties, responsibilities and powers. As leaders in the majority party in their respective houses, they carry considerable weight. Generally, their formal powers include: (1) recognition of members desiring to speak on the floor; (2) appointment of members to committees, both standing and special committees, although to some extent this may be decided in party caucuses; (3) assignment of bills to committees, although this is often determined by custom or legislative rule; and (4) interpretation of the rules of the house or senate. While the formal powers of the presiding officers are similar to those of the presiding officer of any organized group, the informal powers of the speaker or president are determined in large measure by their relative positions and influence in the political party.

Party Leaders. Each party in each house also selects a floor leader to guide the operations of the party on the floor of the respective houses. It is the job of the floor leader to make sure that party members are informed about the legislative calendar, topics of party concern, and party strategy, if any. If a particular bill is to be a party issue, the floor leader is responsible for making this fact known to party members and for insuring their presence at strategic moments in the legislative process.

Committee Chairmen. In Congress committee chairmen are chosen almost solely on the basis of their seniority in the Congress and the respective committees. Seniority as a criterion for selection places the chairman of a committee in a position of power. In state legislatures, however, the seniority rule is less rigid, thus, limiting, to some extent, the power some chairmen from "safe" areas might be able to achieve in particular policy areas as is the case in Congress. While seniority in assigning committee chairmanships is used to some extent in Wyoming, large turnovers in legislative membership and weak party organization has limited considerably the arbitrary power of committee chairmen.

Other Officers and Employees. There are many other legislative posts filled by non-legislative members that are an important source of patronage for the majority party in each house. These positions include a chief clerk, reading clerks, sergeants-at-arms, minute clerks, enrolling and engrossing clerks, attorneys, secretaries, pages, doorkeepers, and a host of others.

The Committee System

Every American legislature has an elaborate system of standing or permanent committees, designed to subdivide the work of the legislature in order that all proposals before the legislature may receive some consideration. It would be an impossible task for the legislature as a whole to give serious consideration to the vast number of legislative proposals without some division of labor. The committee system then has been established according to major substantive policy areas for purposes of considering numerous bills simultaneously, collecting information about governmental problems, and making recommendations concerning bills to the whole legislature. Further, the committee system permits a limited amount of specialization, in that members of particular committees are able to concern themselves with particular areas of policy.

Legislative committee members in Wyoming are appointed by the presiding officers of the two houses, usually in consultation, however, with party leaders in each house. Presently, in the state senate there are 16 committees including judiciary; ways and means; revenue; education, health and welfare; public lands, irrigation and agriculture; livestock; corporations and political subdivisions; transportation and highways; mines and minerals; elections and national relations; game and fish; labor and manufacturing; printing; enrolling and engrossing; rules; and journal committee. In the house there are 19 committees following roughly the same general policy areas as in the senate.

In the house, each committee has an average of nine members. Each member of the house serves on at least two and sometimes three different committees. In the senate the average size of each committee is five members and each member is expected to serve on at least two and sometimes three different committees. In each house, a majority of each committee belongs to the majority party in that house, the size of the majority depending upon the size of the majority in the whole house.

In determining committee assignments and areas of specialization in the committee system of the legislature, occupational and educational backgrounds of the members of each house seem to be significant. Attorneys almost invariably are appointed to the judiciary committees. Farmers and ranchers are appointed to those committees that deal with livestock, agriculture, public lands, and related activities.

THE LEGISLATIVE PROCESS

Organizing a legislative body necessarily includes three distinct processes: (1) choosing the officers of the legislature; (2) establishing the committee system including the process of selecting members of the committees; and, (3) determining and adopting the rules of procedure. The first two points have been discussed briefly, and now we turn to the steps involved in the procedure through which a bill becomes a law in the Wyoming state legislature.

The legislative maze through which all pieces of legislation must pass is a tremendously complex array of steps and strategic points, any one of which may be used to frustrate the final passage of a proposal. The process may be broken down into the highly formal, ritualistic deliberative process which is largely invariable, and the more informal strategy which is less well-known and varies from bill to bill depending upon the nature of the support and opposition of groups and members of the legislature at strategic pressure points in the process. The formal steps in the process are easily ascertainable, but the informal processes are not so easily described without some degree of speculation about what "really" goes on.

The formal legislative process is highly ritualistic with a variety of pomp and circumstance seemingly designed to create the image of careful and deliberative scrutiny of every single proposal. Generally, this formal process includes provision for the following steps: (1) introduction and "first reading" of a bill; (2) referral of the bill to an appropriate committee for study, consideration, and recommendation; (3) placement of the bill on the calendar or "general file" (4) consideration by the committee of the whole house; (5) second reading; (6) third reading and final passage; (7) transmission of the bill to the other house for repetition of the same steps; (8) conference committee between the houses to reconcile differences; (9) transmission to the governor for approval, or veto in which case repassage over the veto may be accomplished by a two-thirds majority. Sandwiched among these basic steps are numerous other detailed technical steps which must be performed in order for a bill to become law.

Of these major steps in the passage of a bill the three steps which are the most vital in terms of offering opportunities for determining the final legislative outcome on a bill are: (1) the committee stage; (2) committee of the whole; and, (3) the conference committee.[20] It might be noted here that the "third reading and final passage" stage is also obviously crucial but at that particular point in the process the fate and content of the bill in a particular house is largely determined. The other three stages, however, offer many opportunities for modifying, killing, or passing a bill, the content of which the originator may have some difficulty recognizing.

The Committee Stage

Every bill introduced in either house is normally referred to an appropriate standing committee for study and recommendation. Generally, it might be said that the committee consideration stage is the most important step in the legislative process. Undoubtedly this is true of the national Congress, although in the states, particularly Wyoming, the committee of the whole stage may be at least equally important. In any case the committee system is designed to allow a relatively small number of "experts" or specialists concentrating on a particular area of public policy, to carefully consider all proposals in that policy area. During the time when committees are studying bills referred to them they normally allow interested and affected citizens, groups, and administrative agencies, opportunities to express their views and desires on the pending legislation. Committees are important in the total process in the sense that they may modify or amend a bill considerably and the committee recommendations concerning bills generally are followed by the whole house. Finally, committees are in a position of being able to kill a bill completely since they may make a "do not pass" recommendation which in effect kills the bill. In Wyoming, committees may not "pigeonhole" a bill indefinitely because the rules of the house state a five-day limitation for committee consideration of a bill and the senate rules stipulate "after a reasonable time" bills may be removed from committee by a motion with three seconds.[21] Strict adherence to these discharge rules, however, is seldom the case.

Committee of the Whole

The rules of both house and senate in Wyoming require that every bill prior to final passage be read in each house three different times on three different legislative days.[22] While this rule can be suspended upon a two-thirds vote of the respective houses, the normal procedure is that in none of the so-called readings is the bill read in its entirety. There is a time, however, in the Wyoming legislature, when a bill is read in its entirety, at least theoretically, and this occurs during the so-called committee of the whole. Even here, however, there is some doubt that the bill is always read in full, bill reading clerks having the reputation of being the "fastest readers in the world."

More importantly, the legislative device of "resolving into the committee of the whole" is used in order to facilitate debate under less formal procedural rules. When consideration on the general file of bills is the order of business, the majority floor leader moves that the house or senate resolve into a committee of the whole. Under this procedure the members of the house or senate are relatively free to discuss, debate, and amend a bill without the restrictive rules of normal operation. Furthermore, no permanent records of the proceedings or votes in the committee of the whole are maintained. Legislators are free to speak or vote their minds with the comforting thought that no formal mention of their remarks or votes will be available to critical constituents unless these constituents happen to be observing in the gallery. Many controversial bills have been killed at this stage of the deliberative process with no formal recording of the ayes and nays. In this way important and interested citizens and groups are kept happy in their ignorance of what their representatives actually did. Upon conclusion of the committees of the whole proceedings only final results and recommendations of the committe are reported back to the formal body.

The Conference Committee

In any legislature, one of the most important steps in the legislative process is consideration by a conference committee. When a measure is passed by one house and later amended by the other, the first house may, of course, accept the amendments, but ordinarily the first house does not concur in the amendments and requests appointment of a conference committee to reconcile differences between the two versions of a bill. A conference committee is then appointed by the presiding officers of the two chambers to adjust these differences. The conference committee often strikes amendments, usually compromises, or even writes new sections in the bill. Only rarely is the report of the conference committee to each house not approved by the two houses. The real significance of the committee, and the reason for much criticism of this institution, lies in the fact that most bills are passed by the two houses so near the end of the session that the chambers have little choice but to accept almost whatever recommendation a conference committee may make. Because these committees

legislature, politics, and legislation

are small and hold a life or death hold over legislative bills, they become easy targets for group and citizen pressures.

Conclusion

The Wyoming legislature in 1974 met for the first time in its new annual session format. Instead of only 40 days every two years, the legislature now holds a short budget session in even-numbered years in addition to the regular 40-day session. The annual session, establishment of a staff agency in the Legislative Service Agency, and interim committees on special problems will perhaps overcome some of the criticisms of the national Citizens Conference on State Legislatures which in 1971 ranked the Wyoming Legislature 49th out of 50 state legislatures.

FOOTNOTES

1. *Wyoming Constitution,* Art. III, Sec. 17.
2. *Ibid.,* Art. III, Sec. 18.
3. *Ibid.,* Art. V. Secs. 1, 2, 7, 24, 17, 20, 21, 22.
4. *Ibid.,* Art. VI.
5. *Ibid.,* Art. III, Sec. 10.
6. *Ibid.,* Art. XX, Sec. 1.
7. *Ibid.,* Art. XX, Sec. 3.
8. *Ibid.,* Art. XV, Secs. 4, 5, 6, 12, 15, 16; Art. XVI, Secs. 1, 2, 3, 4, 6.
9. *Ibid.,* Art. XVI, Secs. 9, 10, 11.
10. *Ibid.,* Art. III, Sec. 27.
11. *Ibid.,* Art. II, Sec. 1; Art. III, Sec. 37.
12. 369 U.S. 186 (1962).
13. 84 S. Ct. 526 (1964).
14. 377 U.S. 533 (1964).
15. *Wyoming Constitution,* Art. III, Sec. 3.
16. 240 F. Supp. 247 (D. Wyo. 1964).
17. The basis for this entire section is B. Oliver Walter and Kendall L. Baker, *The Wyoming Legislature: Lawmakers the Public and the Press,* Laramie: Government Research Bureau, University of Wyoming, 1973, Chapter 1.
18. *Wyoming Constitution,* Art. III, Sec. 17.
19. For a general discussion of this point see Malcolm Jewell, *The State Legislature: Politics and Practice,* New York: Random House, Inc., 1962, Chapter 3.
20. For a general discussion of similar points see Clyde F. Snider, *American State and Local Government,* New York: Appleton-Century-Crofts, 1950, Chapter VIII.
21. *Rules of the Senate and House of Representatives of the Thirty-eighth State Legislature 1965,* House Rule 40; Senate Rule 64.
22. *Ibid.,* House Rule 10; Senate Rule 21.

CHAPTER FOUR

The Governor, Politics, and Administration

The politics and policies of state government are largely "invisible" as far as the average citizen is concerned, but there is one position that seems to symbolize state government—the office of governor. While in fact he often cannot be classified as the chief of state affairs in the same sense that the President dominates national affairs, he occupies a position that is at least somewhat familiar to the average citizen.[1] This sort of phenomenon often places the governor in the position of being held responsible for state policies and programs while in fact, because of the general skeptical and distrustful attitude on the part of citizens and legislators toward bureaucracy and executives, he may not at all be in a position to exercise any significant degree of authority and control over state governmental operations.

Throughout the history of this country chief executives generally have been distrusted following the early experiences of the colonists subject to royal governors. This is evidenced in the numerous restrictions on gubernatorial prerogatives in state constitutions and statutes which provide for multiple elective offices, restrictions on tenure, limited appointment and removal powers, numerous boards and commissions, and similar restrictions. While these restrictions are still in existence in many states, it is also a fact that in recent years chief executives at all levels of government have become increasingly more powerful. The complexities and insoluble problems of modern government and society apparently have created a demand on the part of the public for more effective leadership. The governor, therefore, is in a position, as symbolic chief of state, if not actual leader, to benefit from this demand.

THE OFFICE OF GOVERNOR

Legal Requirements and Availability

In every state there are legal regulations prescribing the qualifications for holding the office of governor. In Wyoming the constitution indicates that he must be a citizen of the United States and a qualified elector of Wyoming, 30 years of age, and a resident of the state for at least five years preceding his election.[2] As is the case with the President of the United States, these legal prerequisites seem to be far less important then considerations of "availability."

There has always been a great deal of speculation among students of government and active politicians as to what constitutes "availability," or appeal to voters, including such characteristics as "pleasing personality," ability to speak well, leadership, honesty, frugality, and other such personal traits. Such nebulous factors, however, are difficult to assess and evaluate. The voters of Wyoming, in selecting 27 different candidates for governor, do indicate some definite considerations that are seemingly important:[3]

> <u>Previous state-level political experience</u>—23 of 27 governors had previous political experience in some state-level governmental position.
> <u>Local political experience</u>—19 of 27 governors had previously held at least one local political office.
> <u>Residence in state</u>—governors average over 32 years of instate residence prior to election, with 11 of the occupants of the position residing in Cheyenne prior to their election.
> <u>Education</u>—23 of 27 governors had at least a university or college education.
> <u>Party affiliation</u>—17 of 27 governors were Republican, ten were Democrats.
> <u>Occupation</u>—nine governors were ranchers (33 per cent) and seven were lawyers (26 per cent), while the remaining 40 per cent were divided among education, business, medicine, banking, engineering, dentistry, press.
> <u>Military experience</u>—since 1931, nine of 12 governors have had military experience, while prior to that time only three of 15 were in the armed forces.
> <u>Age</u>—average age of all governors at the time of inauguration is 53.3 years.

Such other personal factors as religion, Masonic, and fraternal affiliation might also be mentioned although there is no definite trend in relation to these factors.

Tenure, Compensation and Perquisites

In comparison with most other states the governor of Wyoming is in a strong position because of the length of term and tenure provisions of the state constitution. The constitution specifies a four-year term with no restrictions on the number of terms that he may serve.[4] This strength of position, however, is somewhat deceiving since only Governor Hathaway in the history of the state has completed two full terms. Only five governors have been elected twice and two of these were selected once to finish an unexpired term of a previous governor. Only three governors have served as long as six years in office, none of whom has served in the last 15 years. This tradition of limited tenure seems to have had some adverse effect on the over-all policy leadership by the governor serving for a relatively long period of time.

Other than not being re-elected, the governor's office may be vacated by death, resignation, inability to serve, absence from the state or impeachment. In case the office is vacant, the secretary of state serves as the acting governor until the vacancy is filled. The constitution provides that the legislature may impeach and remove the governor from office before his term has expired, although no governor of Wyoming has ever been impeached much less removed from office.[5]

The job of governor is often a costly venture and many states now are beginning to realize this fact. In Wyoming the chief executive is paid $25,000.

He is also provided with the use of the executive mansion, an automobile or an airplane when on "state business," and a small staff with which he is expected to conduct the affairs of the state. In relation to the other states of the union on these matters, Wyoming would probably rank among the "average."

THE ROLES OF THE GOVERNOR[6]

In addition to its being an office occupied by a specific individual, the governorship is an institution. As a result the governor, not unlike the President, is expected to play many social, political, and technical roles in order to meet the expectations not only of the citizens of the state, but other officials of government as well. Publicly, of course, the governor must perform all the expected roles even though this might ordinarily be physically impossible in reality for an ordinary man without the help of a staff, political party, and other administrative leaders. In the end then it is the governor who represents the total institution of the governorship. He must be Chief of State, Chief Executive, Chief Legislator, Chief of Party, Chief Federal Officer, and Chief Board Member all at once and separately if the occasion calls for it.

Chief of State

Much of the work of the governor might be classified as being largely symbolic and ritualistic. As the chief ceremonial representative of the people, he serves as a symbol of the state and is expected to participate in a great variety of sacrosanct and secular rituals in the name of the state and citizenry. Like the President of the United States, he is expected to dedicate new highways; make appearances at yearly conventions; unearth the first shovel of dirt at various groundbreaking ceremonies; meet with civic, church, or school organizations; speak to Boys State and Girls State delegates; grant interviews to a variety of individuals or visiting dignitaries; act as honored guest on the banquet circuit; greet and entertain visiting foreign dignitaries; ride on the Treagle train and in various parades; and perform numerous other such "significant" activities. He is asked to issue proclamations, write letters, and deliver speeches for every conceivable special day, week, or month.

For example, former Governor Hansen's summer, 1965, schedule included the following activities: attended Wyoming Stockgrowers convention, commencement exercises at the university, Third Annual Wyoming Space Age Conference in Riverton, Lovell's 75th Anniversary celebration parade, and Statehood Day ceremonies in Cheyenne; presented the Psychiatric Aide of the Year award in Evanston; addressed the First Annual Labor Seminar in Casper; dedicated the new Colter School building at the Industrial Institute in Worland, the new Hot Springs State Park headquarters in Thermopolis, the Youth Opportunity Center in Casper, and the creation of a new county-wide college district at Western Wyoming Community College in Rock Springs.[7]

Participation in such rituals and symbolic activities by the governor are time-consuming and physically exhausting, but they must be done. Much of the governor's power and prestige, as in the case of the President, are based on faithful performance of these seemingly insignificant details. Through the vehicle of the Chief of State role the governor is able to build a following and a favorable image or atmosphere for accomplishing many of his more difficult and important jobs.

Chief Executive

The Wyoming constitution states explicity that the "executive power" of the state "shall be vested" in the governor and he "shall take care that the laws be faithfully executed."[8] Although the constitution grants these seemingly broad powers to the governor, it subsequently places a great number of rather severe restrictions and limitations on the executive and administrative powers of the Chief Executive. In general terms the executive prerogatives of the governor are not unlike those of the President, but specifically he is in a rather "weak" executive position as compared with the possibilities at the President's command. As Chief Executive, the governor has powers of appointment and removal, personnel supervision and budget control, pardoning and clemency, and is commander-in-chief of the National Guard of the state.

Appointment and Removal. One of the most important functions of any chief executive is the appointment and removal of subordinates within the administrative structure. Ordinarily it would be assumed that the governor would be in a relatively strong position with regard to the selection of personnel in state administration, and although the state constitution and statutes provide for gubernatorial appointment and removal powers, there are also many limitations on this power.

In recent years the governor ordinarily makes in excess of 100 major appointments during a biennium. These appointments, however, are subject to a number of statutory, constitutional, and informal limitations. First, there are four other elective officers, who, along with the governor, serve on boards and commissions responsible for many of the major functions performed in the state. Second, there are many members of other boards and commissions appointed by the governor but who serve longer terms than he does. Third, a number of the chief administrators of major state departments are selected, not by the governor, but by the supervisory board or commission imposed on that department. Fourth, there are many statutory requirements which severely limit the governor's discretion in selecting board members, including such things as representation of both political parties on the board, professional group representation, or geographical representation. Finally, most of the major appointments made by the governor must be confirmed by the state senate. With these limitations on his appointment power, the governor's position in this matter is not comparable to the President's.

The governor can remove any state official that he appoints within limits set by the legislature. His removal authority applies whether the appointment required senate approval or not. Statutory limitations, however, require that the governor may only remove for malfeasance, misfeasance, or nonfeasance, and reasons for removal must be filed with the Secretary of State.

Personnel Supervision and Budgeting. Theoretically, the chief executive is responsible for supervising and controlling the administrative operations and activites of the state government. Whether in fact the governor is the primary director of state activities or not, he is often held responsible by the people for such actions by officials of state government. As already mentioned, he is often limited in his appointment and removal power and thus may not have an effective tool for directing the affairs of certain departments. His status, prestige, or popularity in the state, however, may be a determining factor in whether or not he can expect to receive the cooperation and compliance for which he asks.

Many agencies of state government are not under the governor's exclusive direction. There are four other elective officials who control the affairs of their own departments. There are constitutional and statutory boards and commissions over which he has little control. Finally, some agencies are able to control appointment and removal of their own personnel, and other agencies are completely financially independent because of earmarked sources of revenue. All these factors limit the governor's discretion in directing and supervising state personnel.

The governor is the chief budgetary officer of the state and as such has some control over activities of several of the agencies, at least those that operate out of what is known as the "General Fund." Of course, there are several independent agencies such as the Game and Fish Commission and the Highway Department that are completely free from budgetary control or supervision. Outside of such independent agencies, the governor is responsible for preparing estimates and proposals concerning possible expenditures and income, revising and editing the total state outlay, for submission to the legislature for approval. The legislature may, at its discretion, and often does, modify such gubernatorial proposals, but the governor's proposals generally carry a great deal of weight. Through his budgeting authority, then, the governor is able to direct in some ways the operations of certain state agencies. Again, however, there are these agencies such as Game and Fish and Highway Department, which are not only outside of the fiscal reaches of the governor, but to a large degree outside of direction of even the legislature in their financial and operating procedures. These problems and inaccessible agencies make over-all supervisory, directory, and planning powers of the governor and even the legislature somewhat limited in scope. In 1971, the creation of the Department of Administration and Fiscal Control has provided the Governor with a number of controls in budgeting, personnel, training, purchasing, and supervision that previously did not exist.

Pardoning and Clemency Powers. One of the historical functions of chief executives is the authority to act as kind of a "court of last resort" for individuals punished by the courts. This somewhat distasteful and difficult job of the governor, however, has been modified considerably in recent years through the use of such "modern" concepts as probation, parole, and the indeterminate sentence.

The state constitution specifies that the governor has the power to "remit fines and forfeitures, to grant reprieves, commutations and pardons after conviction, for all offenses except treason and cases of impeachment..."[9] Except for these two limitations and the fact that the legislature may prescribe the manner in which applications for clemency may be accomplished, the authority of the governor is absolute. He also serves on a state board composed of the five elective officers which is responsible for making recommendations concerning clemency.

Commander-in-Chief. The governor is the commander-in-chief of the military forces (National Guard) of the state except when they are called into the service of the United States.[10] Although the state militia was originally probably intended to act as a law-enforcing agency, in Wyoming it has rarely served this purpose. The guard has been used in a number of emergencies such as forest fires and other disaster relief roles but as a state military agency it has largely been inactive except in times of national emergency. Some critics have even questioned the expense and usefulness of such a military force in the nuclear age but the guard, through various influential people, has maintained itself as an on-going agency of state government, albeit an expensive one.

Chief Legislator

Many observers of the state governmental scene have noted over the years that, in most of the states, there has been an increase in the prestige and power of the governor at the expense of the legislature. This increase can partially be explained by the failure of early legislatures to meet their responsibilities, with the result that electorates tended to lose faith in legislative bodies, and partially by the tremendous increase in the complexities of modern society and problems with which governments have to deal. The expansion of many of the original functions of state government, as well as the addition of new ones, has led to vast administrative structures in most states. These complex situations oftentimes are beyond the comprehension of part-time legislators.

Because he is responsible for the actions of the entire administration, the governor is in a much better position than the legislature to assess the over-all problems of state government. These factors tend to stimulate gubernatorial leadership in policy formation. Governors, on the whole, also have tended to emphasize legislative relations, for in their bids for re-election they can gain more political advantage by stressing their policy achievements rather than administrative management successes.[11]

Granted the importance of the governor's role in policy formation, especially in relation to the legislature, what sorts of informal techniques can he be expected to use in order to adequately carry out his role in the policy-making process? Informally, he uses the power of persuasion, his role as party leader, periodic conferences with legislative leaders, threat of the veto, government contracts, political patronage, and, as a last resort, an appeal to the electorate for public support of his proposals. Formally, his legislative powers include messages to the legislature, the veto, the budget, and calling special sessions.

Messages and Policy Innovation. In 48 states the governor is authorized to recommend a program to the legislature in a manner patterned after the United States Constitution which provides that the President " . . . shall from time to time give to the Congress Information of the State of the Union, and recommend to their Consideration such Measures as he shall judge necessary and expedient."[12] This authority is the basis for the policy-forming function of the governor, giving him an opportunity to present a program to the legislature. In 23 states, including Wyoming, this "state of the state" message can be supplemented by subsequent messages from time to time during the legislative session.[13]

Policy innovation through the messages to the legislature, however, often depends upon the individual who holds the office of governor. As has been the case with the office of President, some Wyoming governors have appeared to be strong leaders and others relatively weak. According to their messages to the legislature, which, of course, are not a completely accurate measure of leadership, some governors have made many and vigorous recommendations, while others seem to have been content to allow the legislative branch to follow its own course. Since 1950, with one two-year exception, relatively vigorous gubernatorial leadership in the legislature seems to have been the rule. Governors during this period made many ambitious proposals and suggestions to the legislature with a relatively large degree of success. Establishment of the natural resource board in 1950 was largely a legislative implementation of the governor's proposals. The creation of a centralized Revenue Department occured mainly through the efforts of the governor. Establishment and implementation of a vigorous stream pollution council and a major study of state administration with some resulting revamping occurred through the governor's insistence. Throughout the history of the state, it seems that many of the major policies and administrative changes have occurred through the insistence of the governor, even though by most administrative standards, the governor of Wyoming is considered relatively "weak."

Budget Making. Closely related to the governor's duty to present messages to the legislature is his responsibility to recommend a budget for the next fiscal period. In 42 states, including Wyoming, the governor is directly responsible for the budget, sharing this power with a board or a commission in only eight states.[14] The budget supposedly is a comprehensive and systematic financial plan for the coming fiscal year, indicating the proposed expenditures and revenues. The budget power of the governor is somewhat deceiving, however, for a closer examination of the budget indicates that it actually covers only a relatively small part of the state's income and expenditures. Since the majority of the state's income are in the form of "earmarked" revenues, for specific agencies or functions, the budget only covers the general fund which involves only approximately 25-30 per cent of the total state income and expenditures.

Special Sessions. The convening of special sessions of the legislatures in the several states is typically at the exclusive discretion of the governor. In all states the governor can call the special session; in 22 states, but not Wyoming, he may even limit the subjects to be considered by the special session to those that he designates in the call; and, in only 14 states, but not Wyoming, can the legislature call itself into session.[15] Because of the biennial sessions of the legislatures in most states, there has been a considerable increase in the use of the special session in recent years, although Wyoming governors have not used this technique frequently.

The Veto Power. As a last resort the governor has at his command the use of the executive veto in all of the states except North Carolina. This negative power has been used effectively by most governors to emphasize the importance of their legislative program and to frustrate hasty legislation. The effectiveness of the gubernatorial veto is illustrated by the fact that less than two per cent are usually overridden.[16]

There are four vital elements that can be distinguished in the veto power of the governor: the extraordinary majority in the legislature which is needed to override a veto; the time that the governor is allowed to consider bills presented to him; the ability of the governor to withhold his signature and thus deny passage to a bill (the pocket veto); and, the governor's prerogative in disapproving specific items in appropriations without invalidating the entire bill (item veto).[17] A combination of all four elements would give the governor an exceedingly strong veto power. Most state constitutions, however, do not give their governor all four of these prerogatives, at least not in this form.

Nearly all the state constitutions demand some form of extraordinary majority to override the governor's veto. Wyoming falls into the group of states (24) which demand a two-thirds vote of those *elected* to membership to override the governor's veto.[18] This group of states gives the governor an extremely strong veto power—a check more powerful than the President holds over Congress.

The time that the governor has to consider bills can be an important factor in his veto power, especially as the legislative session moves to a close. Since legislatures pass most bills near the end of the session, the longer the governor has to consider a bill the more likely it is that the legislature will have already adjourned at the expiration of his time limit. If the legislature has already adjourned, the veto power of the governor becomes absolute. This time limit varies considerably in the 50 states, from a minimum of three days to a maximum of 45 days. In Wyoming, the governor has three days to consider bills if the legislature is still in session and 15 days if it is adjourned.[19]

The pocket veto, or the negation of a bill after legislative adjournment by inaction on the part of the governor, has not achieved great popularity in the states. Only 17 governors have the pocket veto, not including Wyoming. A much more popular provision in state constitutions is the item veto, through which the governor may strike specific items from appropriation measures without negating the entire bill. Forty-one states, including Wyoming, have this authority of the governor written into the constitution.[20] It has not been used with any degree of regularity, however, in Wyoming.

Executive-Legislative Relations. Historically, the legislature, especially the senate, has been controlled primarily by the Republican party. During the 80-year period of statehood from 1890-1970, the Democratic party controlled the house of representatives on only five occasions (ten years), and the senate only twice (four years). During two legislative sessions the membership of the house was equally divided between Republicans and Democrats and in one session neither major party had a majority. (See Table 4.) This situation is comparable to that which exists in the administrative branch where the Democrats have controlled membership on administrative boards only five different biennial periods (ten years) during the 80-year history of the state.

Republican dominance in the legislative branch and on administrative boards has meant that when the governor's office is controlled by the Democratic party, the legislature and most of the state administration is still controlled by the opposite party. Although more Republicans have captured the office of governor during the years of statehood, the Democrats have regularly had at least an even chance of capturing the office. The Republicans hold a 17-10 edge during the entire period from 1890 to the present. The Democratic governors, when elected, have had a majority of both houses Democratic only during one four-year period in the 1930's. At other times when Democratic governors have been elected, at least one or both houses have been controlled by the opposition. Republican governors, on the other hand, have never been opposed in both houses by Democratic majorities, and only once has a Republican governor been faced by as much as an opposition majority in one house and on one occasion a Republican governor faced a tie in one house. (See Table 14.)

Chief of Party

Virtually every other role of the governor is closely related to his role as chief of the political party. If he is a good administrator, presents a vigorous and successful program to the legislature, performs magnificently as chief of state, and successfully promotes and defends the position of the state in its external

TABLE 14
Party Control and Executive—Legislative Relations in Wyoming, 1890-1974

Type of Relationship	No. of Years	Per Cent of the Period
Governor and a Majority of Both Houses of the Legislature of the Same Party	52	61.9
Democratic Governor and Legislature	4	4.8
Republican Governor and Legislature	48	57.1
Governor Faced by a Majority of the Opposite Party in One House of the Legislature	12	14.3
Democratic Governor— Republican Opposition	8	9.5*
Republican Governor— Democratic Opposition	4	4.8*
Governor Faced by a Majority of the Opposite Party in Both Houses of the Legislature	20	23.8
Democratic Governor— Republican Opposition	20	23.8
Republican Governor— Democratic Opposition	0	0.0
TOTALS	84	100.0	100.0

*Includes two ties in house of representatives and one session with no majority party in house of representatives.

affairs, his position as titular, if not actual, head of his political party will be strengthened.

The political task of the governor is closely akin to his job as chief of state, in that he must perform innumerable ceremonial tasks relative to party activities as well as for the entire citizenry. As chief of his political party, the governor is expected to attend rallies, dinners, picnics, and conventions of the senior or junior party. He is ultimately responsible for distribution of patronage and party policy leadership both in the legislature and in the administration. During the campaign, of course, whether he is running for office or not, he is expected to participate with real or apparent enthusiasm in the endorsement and encouragement of his party's candidates for every conceivable office on the national and local tickets. His performance, or lack of it as party chieftain is fraught with difficulties, and frustrations, and problems, but again, as in the case of his role as chief of state, it is a job that must be done in order to successfully accomplish his other tasks.

Chief Federal Officer

The discussion to this point has described some of the salient features of the governor's role within the state, his relations with the legislature and the administration. It must not be overlooked, however, that the governor of Wyoming is necessarily involved in many "federal" affairs, and, not dissimilar to the role of the President as Chief Foreign Policy Maker, is responsible for the relations of the state with other states and the national government. One scholar points out: "It follows therfore that gubernatorial power is and must be partially a product of the 'federal' status of the office of governor."[21] The governor often finds himself in the position of not only "administering" state policy, but defending, promoting, advising, condemning, and approving "federal" relationships involving the state of Wyoming.

From territorial days through statehood to the present the most often played role of the governor has been that of the "liaison" man among state, local, and national officials. In some instances the governor has played the role of promoter of national action in the state. For example, in 1873, Governor Campbell pleaded with the legislature to adopt a memorial to Congress "setting forth our wants and necessities in regard to this matter (irrigation), and praying for governmental aid and assistance in some national plan of irrigation."[22] In 1895 Governor Richards asked the legislature to memorialize Congress "asking that the headwaters of every important stream in the State and under National control be set aside as a forest reserve," which would be of "incalculable benefit to the arid States."[23] In 1927, while decrying "federal intervention" (see below), Governor Emerson stated in the legislature:

> The Federal Government is engaged upon the construction and settlement of three large irrigation projects in this State. This development is very desirable and due credit should be given the Government for the valuable additions that have been made possible to the taxable assets of the State. In recent years, however, it is my opinion that Wyoming has not been dealt with in the matter of appropriations for its projects... To the plan announced by the Interior Department, Wyoming should make a vigorous protest...[24]

In 1955, Governor Simpson suggested: "State legislation making it possible for the State, through the board (Natural Resource Board), to take advantage of any Federal legislation to aid our State in financing so-called smaller projects (water projects), also is essential."[25] In 1965 Governor Hansen led a team of state citizens and officials in attempting to lure a proposed giant atomic accelerator to the state of Wyoming. These are but a few examples of the promotional activities of the governor.

On the other hand, the governor is often required in his role as Chief Federal Officer, to act as the "defender" of the state when in opposition to the programs and policies of the national government or other states. This role has been assumed by nearly every individual who has held this office regardless of political party affiliation. It is probably dictated by the vast amount of federal land and involvement in the state's affairs. Shortly after statehood was achieved, the role became clearly defined and governor after governor has directed his invectives and demands of withdrawal upon the "bureaucratic devils" in Washington.

The most bitter attacks on the national government's role often concern the public lands and water rights in the state. Governor Brooks was particularly disturbed:

> *Unfortunately, the present policy relative to the conservation, of this (water resources), like other natural resources, seems to be to accomplish all reforms through federal agencies. The limelight is all on the national stage. Reforms and good policies are not to be struggled for at home, but are to be placed in the hands of federal departments, whose chiefs are over-anxious to strengthen their departments, and as they are not acquainted with local conditions, their meddlesome activity frequently acts as a hindrance to our development, and hence irritates our people.*[26]

Twenty years later, Governor Emerson, a Republican, was also apprehensive of the growth of the national government under the Republican administrations of the 1920's:

> *There is a growing tendency toward centralization of power in bureaus and departments in Washington. This tendency marks continuing infringement upon state rights and I believe that we should resist with vigor...*
>
> *... the Federal Government has the tendency to reach out for further control over our natural resources. Believing this general policy to be adverse to the interests of the State and its development, I am convinced that we should oppose further extension of Federal control in the State except in instances where the aid and cooperation of the Federal Government would appear of benefit.*[27]

Every governor since that time has reiterated the charges of "federal intervention."

The United States Constitution also makes it obligatory for the governor of a state to return fugitives from another state to that state for trial. While the governor's role in the extradition of criminals appears obligatory, in practice governors have used their discretion in determining whether to send fugitives back to another state for trial depending upon the circumstances involved in the particular case. There are many instances of governors refusing to return to the state of origin individuals apprehended in their respective states.

The governor's role as Chief Federal Officer is illustrated in such activities as testifying on behalf of the state before congressional committees, receiving briefings from the State Department on foreign affairs, participating in such strictly "federal" affairs as national defense through his role as commander-in-chief of the National Guard of the state, and attending national and regional conferences and meetings on such diverse topics as water resources, interstate oil compacts, regional development, education, and other similar activities.

Finally, the governor's "federal" role is brought to light in his dealings with other state governors, whether in the National Governor's Conference or the Western Governor's Conference. For a number of years the western governors have attempted to play a role in promoting and defending policies involving the use and development of the West's natural resources. Also, the governors of the Upper Colorado River Basin states (Colorado, New Mexico, Utah, and Wyoming) periodically meet to discuss their mutual water and resource problems.

Chief Board Member

The fact that the governor is a member of many and varied boards and commissions has already been mentioned but it deserves some special attention. Much of the governor's time and effort is taken up with this rather mundane activity. Instead of being chief administrator, in many instances he is just one of many other board members, sometimes the chairman of this or that commission, other times merely an "ex officio member without vote." He is expected to be well versed in diverse subjects to the point of making technical judgements as a member of an agency's governing body. This expertise may include agricultural policy, liquor purchasing, public welfare, parole and probation, state deposits, farm loans, oil and gas conservation, and recreation. Even boards of which he is not a member cannot escape his watchful eye. Within thirty days after a state election the State Canvassing Board, composed of the Secretary of State, State Auditor, and State Treasurer, must meet in the "presence of the Governor" and he "observes" while the board canvasses the vote for electors, state officers, supreme court justices, senators and representatives.

As mentioned elsewhere, the governor must serve on a total of 22 boards and commissions which make up the bulk of state administration. It would seem that his time could be used in much more economical fashion. Several "insiders" in Cheyenne have noted that many of the commissions and boards only meet formally while the governor is present, and they "get their work done" after he leaves to go to another board meeting. It would appear that the governor has far too many more important duties with which he is entrusted to spend time attending formal rituals.

DIVIDED ADMINISTRATION

The governor, as performer of various roles described in the previous section, is however, not free from a number of limitations established by the constitution and statutes, although the degree of leadership exhibited by any particular individual, of course, seems to vary according to the incumbent's individual conception of the duties of the office and the political environment in which he must work. The governor's appointive and removal powers, and his supervisory powers over the executive branch, are limited by the fact that he is only one of five elective officials who comprise a large number of the boards and commissions that have been established to direct most of the major operations of state government in Wyoming. Although the governor is officially the "chief" administrative officer of the state, the Secretary of State, State Auditor, State Treasurer, and State Superintendent of Schools are also elected statewide. These five officials serve ex officio on 14 boards of which the governor is chairman, ranging from the State Canvassing Board to the State Liquor Commission. The governor is also a member of eight other boards on which he is not the chairman, ranging from the Board of Agriculture to the University of Wyoming Board of Trustees, for a grand total of membership on 22 boards and commissions. In addition the governor appoints members to 12 major boards and commissions, 15 professional examining boards and commissions, and 22 major officers of government ranging from the attorney general to state water commissioners. All of these appointees serve definite terms, most of which do not correspond with the governor's. According to the count of one governor, Wyoming has 76 state agencies, composed of 33 major departments, and 43 other agencies, in addition to 16 boards within departments.[28] Thus, some state officials are elected, some are appointed by the governor and some by other officials, and some are ex officio.

The fact that the governor's administrative control is divided means that even though the office of governor is closely contested by both major political parties, party control of the other elective offices assumes a great deal of meaning. The four other major state-wide elective offices, as is the case with the legislature, have been controlled primarily by members of the Republican party. The Republicans have controlled *all five* of the elective offices 42 years during the 84-year history of the state, while the Democrats have captured all five major offices only one four-year period during the 1930's. The Democratic party has controlled a majority of the five offices (3-2) for a period of ten years during Wyoming's history, the Republicans having a majority 26 years. The Republicans, thus, have controlled all or a majority of the offices for a total of 68 years, and one two-year period was evenly divided after a gubernatorial resignation. Only five of 20 Secretaries of State, three of 20 State Auditors, four of 20 Superintendents of Public Instruction, and one of 22 State Treasurers have been members of the Democratic party. The upshot of this is that while the two parties regularly contest evenly for the governorship, a Democrat is likely to be only a member of an opposition team in "administering" the affairs of the state.

The fragmentation and disintegration of the state administration in Wyoming is the result of many "natural" phenomena and pressures over the years. The structure of state government specified by the constitution, which indicates the major elective and several appointive offices, is difficult to change. Realigning responsibilities and functions of certain agencies is difficult to accomplish because of interest group involvement with these agencies. Also, many students of administrative organization point out that it is natural for agencies to develop self-interest attitudes and strive for independence and autonomy. Closely related to this is the modern-day trend toward professionalism in the governmental service. Apparently this is no longer the day of the political hack and patronage for complex and technical problems of government demand professional competence. This natural tendency means that such professions as engineering, law, forestry, game and fish management, and many others develop professional codes of ethics and respond to functional cues rather than central "political" direction. With these significant reasons for non-reorganization, plus a general legislative and popular distrust of centralized control of administration, reform movements of the past have not accomplished the major changes they had anticipated. Many organization theorists emphasize that such reform movements, even when accomplished, rarely result in changing the patterns of social, professional, and political relationships which have been set up over a period of time. Changing of desks, promotion, demotion, cause surface changes for a short time, but subsequent study indicates a return to much the same patterns as developed previously with little substantial substantive change.

Thus, gubernatorial leadership in Wyoming administration is likely to be a process of bargaining with party leaders, uncoordinated administrative officials, interested pressure groups, and professionals. Undoubtedly, the governor's bargaining power is limited by the fragmented constitutional structure, and any gubernatorial leadership is largely personal achievement and perseverance rather than a result of hierarchical authority.

FOOTNOTES

1. A recent survey of citizens in Wyoming, for example, illustrated this in that policies, programs, and lesser state officials were generally unknown to the respondents, but 96 per cent of those questioned were able to correctly identify the governor.
2. *Wyoming Constitution,* Art. IV, Sec. 2.
3. The following data were compiled and analyzed in John Hursh, "Availability Factor Trends and the Office of Governor in Wyoming," (paper prepared for the Department of Political Science, University of Wyoming), January 1965.
4. *Wyoming Constitution,* Art. IV, Sec. 1.
5. *Ibid.,* Art. III, Sec. 17.
6. Similar analysis of the President's roles is used in Clinton Rossiter, *The American Presidency,* New York: The New American Library of World Literature, Inc., 1956.
7. *Wyoming GOP Trunkline,* Vol. 5, No. 7, July, 1965.
8. *Wyoming Constitution,* Art. IV, Secs. 1, 4.
9. *Ibid.,* Art. IV, Sec. 5; remitting a fine means returning the money paid as a fine to the individual making the payment; full pardons absolve the convicted individuals in the eyes of the law and restore their political rights and privileges while conditional pardons may be granted in which case the governor specifies certain conditions to be adhered to by the individual receiving the pardon; reprieve involves postponement of the execution of a sentence; and, commutation involves reduction of a sentence.
10. *Ibid.,* Art. IV, Sec. 4.
11. Coleman B. Ransone, Jr., *The Office of Governor in the United States,* University, Alabama: University of Alabama Press, 1956, page 142; also see Karl A. Bosworth, "Law Making in State Governments," *The Forty-eight States: Their Tasks as Policy Makers and Administrators,* New York: The American Assembly, 1955, page 105.

12. *United States Constitution,* Art. II, Sec. 3.
13. Legislative Drafting Research Fund of Columbia University, *Index Digest of State Constitutions,* (2nd Edition), New York: Oceana Publications, Inc., 1959, pages 503-504.
14. Ransone, *op. cit.,* page 165.
15. *The Book of the States, 1960-1961,* Vol. XIII, Chicago: The Council of State Governments, 1960, pages 40-41.
16. Ransone, *op. cit.,* page 213.
17. Frank W. Prescott, "The Executive Veto in American States," *The Western Political Quarterly,* Vol. III, March, 1950, page 99.
18. *The Book of the States, 1960-1961, op. cit.,* page 51.
19. *Wyoming Constitution,* Art. IV, Sec. 8.
20. *Ibid.,* Art. IV, Sec. 9.
21. Thomas J. Anton, "Gubernatorial Leadership and Federal Funds: Three Cases," in Institute of Government and Public Affairs, University of Illinois, *Assembly on the Office of Governor,* (mimeo), Allerton Park, Illinois, December 6-7, 1962, page 1.
22. *Message of Governor Campbell to the Third Legislative Assembly of Wyoming Territory, 1873,* page 7.
23. *Message of William A. Richards, Governor of Wyoming, to the Third Legislative Assembly, 1895,* page 23.
24. *Message of Governor Frank C. Emerson to the Nineteenth State Legislature of Wyoming, 1927,* pages 18-19.
25. *Message Delivered to the Thirty-third Session Wyoming Legislature, 1955, by Governor Milward L. Simpson,* page 15.
26. *Message of Bryant B. Brooks, Governor of Wyoming, to the Tenth State Legislature, 1909,* page 30.
27. *Message of Governor Frank C. Emerson to the Nineteenth State Legislature of Wyoming, 1927,* page 18.
28. *Message Delivered to the Thirty-fourth Session Wyoming Legislature, 1957, by Milward L. Simpson, Governor,* page 12.

CHAPTER FIVE

The State Judicial System

Despite the fact that sooner or later many citizens will probably be involved in some type of judicial action, whether a minor traffic case or a major civil or criminal suit, most citizens know less about the judicial branch of government than they do about the legislature or administration. Although the average individual is probably at least vaguely aware that courts exist in the state, the inner workings and hidden mechanisms of court structure, lawyers, judges, bailiffs, prosecutors, plaintiffs are largely symbolic in meaning rather than real. Undoubtedly, most people probably even believe that our government is "a government of laws, not of men," and that state courts are the instruments through which this is accomplished.

The Wyoming state court system in 1972 experienced two major changes as a result of the approval by the voters of a constitutional change in the method of selection of judges. Subsequently the legislature also made some changes in the structure of the lower courts.

THE ROLE OF THE COURTS

The court is the governmental institution designed to provide for peaceful solution of disputes concerning matters of law. It is often said that the legislature determines general governmental policy, the executive carries out or executes the law, and when specific disputes or controversies arise, the courts provide a neutral mechanism for solving the problem. In our system the court attempts to determine what the law actually is and applies it to the facts in a specific case.

Types of Law

The "law" to be determined by the court may actually take several forms. In this country there is the "higher law" of the constitution. Except in Louisiana, state courts generally adhere to the English common-law tradition where applicable. Common law is judge-made law stemming historically from local customs, traditions, church teachings, local practices, and past decisions of judges. Over the centuries such law tended to harden as precedents developed and fixed legal patterns emerged. As a result of this tendency, another type of judge-made law developed which is called equity or so-called "natural justice." This type of law is based not only on the "law" and strict legal precedent, but also on the peculiar facts in a particular case. Finally, in the last 100 years or so, legislatures have codified many of these precedents in the form of statutory law.

Controversies before a court for settlement fall into two general classes, civil and criminal. A civil case usually involves a dispute between two private persons, although in certain instances the government itself may be classified as a private person. Frequently, civil cases are begun in an effort of one individual to seek redress from another for a private wrong (as distinguished from a public wrong or crime). The state itself has no particular interest in the case other than providing the judicial machinery for peaceful settlement of the private dispute. Civil suits might include such matters as breach of contract, property rights, divorces, and torts.

Criminal cases, on the other hand, always involve public wrongs. Statutes define public wrongs or crimes which are considered dangerous to the public welfare and set penalties for infractions. Most public wrongs are usually acts against individuals, such as murder, burglary, and arson, but are so serious that they constitute wrongs against the state and society itself. Actually crimes, as defined by the legislature, range in seriousness from minor infractions (misdemeanors) to serious crimes, called felonies. In criminal cases the state acts as the prosecutor and the court's function is to determine if possible whether the accused person actually committed the alleged infraction, and if so determined, set the penalty.

Judicial Policy-making

Certainly most of the decisions by courts in specific cases could be classified as strictly routine in their significance for the general political system. While not without some importance, divorces, probates, and traffic cases rarely vitally affect the structure of the system. There are, however, certain judicial decisions which do significantly affect the structures and functions of the political system. For example, one of the most significant functions of the courts is that of judicial review. Constitutions are considered to be "supreme law of the land" in each governmental jurisdiction, state or nation, and courts have assumed the general responsibility of passing on the validity of legislative or administrative acts involved in cases actually before them in relation to the "higher law," or constitution, which is deemed binding on both the court and the legislature. In so ruling, a court may actually interpret the constitution, as there is always an element of choice involved in deciding on the validity of legislative or administrative enactments in relation to such vague constitutional provisions as taxing powers, inter- and intra-state commerce powers, and especially the general police power of the states. Courts, of course, do not exercise this power of judicial review indiscriminately. Courts will decide the validity of statutes only in specific cases and only when there is no other basis for making a decision in a case, and they will not anticipate a constitutional question.

Courts also make many tremendously significant policy decisions which may not involve judicial review, but which have great impact on the political system.

Judges often rationalize that they do not "make" public policy, but only interpret the law and apply it to specific cases. One need only point, however, to three relatively recent United States Supreme Court decisions to demonstrate the policy-making activities of courts. The school desegregation decisions, the cases involving religion in the public schools, and the apportionment decisions are all good examples of policy decisions involving problems which had not been solved by the ordinary processes of state and national "political" branches of government.

Courts are also involved in the political process by virtue of the fact that they are available to interested individuals and groups for purposes of securing individual rights against other governmental branches or agencies. Groups may even use the courts for general discussion of controversial issues or enactments. Issues such as apportionment, right-to-work, segregation, religion in the schools, have received much attention and discussion through group involvement in the judicial process.

Courts may also be involved in the political process through their roles in the enforcement of controversial criminal laws. Prosecutors in some instances have been hesitant about strictly enforcing certain laws involving such problems as gambling, prostitution, liquor control, and closing times because of their significant political overtones. Thus an officer of the court, the prosecuting attorney, may have a great deal of discretion in enforcement of legislative enactments and the court is at least indirectly involved. Judges have also been known to turn the other way, frustrating in some cases the desires of ambitious and overzealous prosecutors or "reformers."

Several studies have shown, for instance, that judges do not automatically discard their political and social preferences by merely donning the judicial robes. Courts then have a very significant role to play in the political system despite some vigorous judicial denials. Judges do not just contemplate the law and in their ultimate wisdom arrive automatically or mechanically at the "truth." The court, therefore, should not be pictured as a mechanical body, composed of lawyer-technicians, dispensing justice according to the "law" whenever a coin is inserted in the automat. This mechanical theory of jurisprudence, plus the apparent apathy and ignorance of the general public about judicial decisions and records, apparently has forestalled the investigation of social and political factors which might actually influence judicial behavior.

JURISDICTION OF STATE COURTS

One of the more important distinguishing features of the court system in the United States is that there are actually two separate and independent systems operating within the total political system. The constitutional division of powers between state and national governments, makes necessary the establishment of two parallel and independent court systems, each having jurisdiction within its own sphere of action. As in the legislative division of powers between Congress and state legislatures (see Chapter Three), the national courts have delegated jurisdiction in particular enumerated types of controversies, and state courts have residual jurisdiction insofar as the state constitution does not prohibit jurisdiction. The national Constitution delegates jurisdiction to national courts in all cases arising under the United States Constitution, laws, treaties, or admiralty law. National courts also have delegated jurisdiction in certain cases depending upon who the parties involved are. National courts, thus, have jurisdiction in enumerated cases such as "cases affecting ambassadors, public ministers and consuls," cases in which the United States government is a party, cases between two states or involving citizens of two different states, or cases involving a state and a citizen of another state.[1] All cases which do not fall under these two constitutionally delegated areas of national judicial concern, come under the jurisdiction of state courts. There are, of course, some cases in which the two levels of courts have concurrent jurisdiction, unless Congress has granted exclusive jurisdiction to the national courts in that field.

Most criminal and civil cases, consequently, fall under the jurisdiction of the state courts. The national government does not have general police powers and state legislatures do. Therefore, state courts are the primary recipients of criminal cases arising under the police power of the state. Further, national courts are not on a higher level than state courts and cases may *not* automatically be appealed from state courts to national courts, unless some federal question is involved. Recent interpretations of the prohibitions on states contained in the Fourteenth Amendment to the United States Constitution have increased the number of cases going to national courts from state courts, since such national guarantees as freedom of religion, speech, press, assembly also apply to states' actions. In most instances, however, state supreme courts are the courts of last resort. As a matter of practice, most cases begin and end in the lowest state courts of general jurisdiction with no appeal to either higher state courts or to national courts.

ORGANIZATION OF THE WYOMING COURTS

The organization and jurisdiction of courts in Wyoming are largely determined by the state constitution, although the legislature has some discretion on details. The constitution and statutes provide for three basic levels of courts in Wyoming. These include: (1) county courts, justice of the peace courts, police, or municipal courts at the lowest level; (2) courts of general trial jurisdiction, or district courts; and, (3) the state supreme court. These three levels of courts are also found in every other state of the union, although most states have various intermediate levels, or at least a far more complex structure than that in Wyoming.

County Courts and Justice of the Peace Courts

The Legislature in 1971 authorized the establishment of County Courts beginning in 1975 to replace the Justice of the Peace courts in the five most populous counties of the state. This was an attempt to upgrade the local court system by providing that a full-time judge will be available at the local level and a salary commensurate with his responsibilities will be paid. The salary was originally set at $15,000 but it would appear that this will not be sufficient to attract well-qualified lawyers. Candidates for the position of county judge must be qualified attorneys. The Attorney General of the state has determined that these judges will be elected rather than appointed by the new appointment system used for district courts and the state supreme court. The jurisdiction of the new court would be similar to that of the justice of the peace courts. The system is mandatory for the larger counties and optional at this time for the other counties.

At the lowest level of the court system in nearly every state is found the justice of the peace. Usually elected, as they are in Wyoming, justices serve in a judicial precinct as created by the board of county commissioners. The jurisdiction of the justice court is limited to specific kinds of cases. First, justices try civil cases in which the amount involved is less than a specified amount ($200 in Wyoming). Second, justices try minor criminal cases or misdemeanors. In Wyoming, cases in which conviction involves a fine of less than $100 or less than six months in county jail, fall into this category. Such cases as those involving traffic violations and disturbing the peace are typical misdemeanors. Third, the justice may hold preliminary hearings in cases involving felonies or serious crimes. Such hearings are held to determine whether or not there is enough evidence to justify holding a suspect for further judicial action.[2] Incidental to their judicial functions, justices of the peace also may perform certain duties of an essentially non-judicial nature such as performing marriages and administering oaths. Decisions of the justice court may be appealed to the district court, although appealed cases are retried by the district court since the justice court is not a court of record.

Substantial criticism of the justice of the peace courts has been made in recent years. In the first place justices ordinarily are not required to be learned in the law. No special training or preparation usually is necessary to becoming a justice of the peace. Surveys of justices show a variety of social and political backgrounds and qualifications. Secondly, the fee system of payment for justices has been almost universally attacked. In Wyoming, the constitution states that legislatively determined salaries must be paid to justices, except those in judicial precincts of less than 1,500 population in which case their only salary is that which can be derived from judicial fees set by the legislature.[3] Income for justices in rural areas then is largely determined by the volume of business which is brought to them. Needless to say, this type of arrangement is hardly conducive to fair and impartial justice. The Wyoming Bar Association has been very critical of the justice court, and was instrumental in having a proposed constitutional amendment placed on the 1964 ballot which would have allowed certain legislative changes to be made. The amendment was defeated. In 1966, however, an amendment to the constitution which would permit the legislature to establish subordinate courts by law was passed although it has not yet been implemented entirely.

At the same level in the state court system as the justice courts are found the municipal or police courts. These courts have jurisdiction over infractions against city ordinances, but with similar restrictions as those imposed on justices of the peace. Judges in these courts are appointed by the mayor of the city in which the court is located. Appeals from the municipal courts may be taken to the district court as is the case with appeals from justice courts.

District Courts

The general trial court in Wyoming is the district court. This court may try civil cases and criminal cases without restrictions as to amounts or seriousness of the offenses involved. Except for the minor cases begun in justice or municipal courts, and these may be appealed to the district court, practically all civil and criminal cases in the state begin in the district court. Thus district courts have both original and appellate jurisdiction.

Of all courts the district court is probably most familiar to the average citizen. This is the court where there is only one judge, usually a jury although it may be dispensed with, prosecutors, defense counsel, witnesses, and all the drama and ritual popularly associated with justice in America.

There are seven judicial districts in Wyoming, each of which has at least one district judge. Judges are popularly elected by voters in the district on a nonpartisan ballot. Each district is composed of three to four counties, and the district judge holds court in each of the counties of the district in turn. At the discretion of the judge, district courts may also serve as juvenile courts in the district.

One final point should be emphasized. For most individuals involved in judicial proceedings, the district courts are courts of last resort. Of the vast number of cases heard each year in general trial courts in the United States, only a very few cases are appealed, or even appealable, to higher courts. While the more important and controversial cases generally are appealed, the vast number of cases are largely routine, and begin and end at the district court level.

Supreme Court

The final interpreter of the state constitution and state laws is the Wyoming supreme court. Unless a federal question is involved, and this is rare, there is no appeal from the state supreme court. The jurisdiction of the Wyoming supreme court is primarily appellate in that it hears cases appealed to it from the district courts and attempts to correct "errors" of the several district courts. The supreme court also has a constitutionally limited amount of original jurisdiction, including the power to issue writs of quo warranto, mandamus, and habeas corpus concerning all state officers.[4] Further, regarding its jurisdiction, the constitution states that the supreme court has power to issue "writs of mandamus, review, prohibition, habeas corpus, certiorari, and other writs necessary and proper to the complete exercise of its appellate and revisory jurisdiction."[5]

Similar to all appellate courts, the operation of the Wyoming supreme court is considerably different than that found in general trial courts. The five members of the court sit as a bench. Juries and witnesses are absent, and the role of the attorney is clearly secondary. Oral and written arguments are presented to the court and the whole atmosphere is quiet and scholarly. Most of the work of the court is done in the judge's study rather than in open court. Decisions are reached after long, scholarly investigation of legal precedents and issued in the form of a written opinion. Decisions are made by majority vote of the five-member court. A judge in the minority may also issue a dissenting opinion and judges who voted with the majority on a decision, but for different reasons than those expressed in the majority opinion of the court, may issue concurring opinions.

THE JUDICIAL PROCESS

The detailed processes and procedures used in the judicial system are rather intricate, technical, and complex, but the fundamental steps involved are relatively simple. In any criminal or civil case the court must determine the facts involved in the case, decide what the law is, and apply the law to the specific facts in order to arrive at a decision in the case. With these three basic processes in mind, we turn now to a brief outline of some of the major steps involved in criminal and civil trials.

Criminal Cases

In a criminal case, the first step is to apprehend and arrest the individual suspected of the alleged infraction. Depending upon the time and nature of the crime, the police officer may have a written warrant from a court indicating why the individual should be arrested. Warrants are not always necessary, however, if the police have reason to believe that immediate arrest is justified, or they actually see an individual committing a crime. Shortly after the arrest, the suspected individual is given a preliminary hearing in a minor or justice of the peace court at which time the justice decides whether there is enough evidence to hold the arrested individual and bind him over for trial, or to release him.

The next step is the making of a formal charge by the county prosecuting attorney. The prosecuting attorney may file an "information" setting forth the specific criminal violations, or this might also be done by a grand jury through indictment. Grand juries are rarely, if ever, used in Wyoming. Next, the accused is arraigned in the district court at which time the information is read to the accused and he is asked to make an oral and general plea to the charges. If the accused does not have legal counsel, or is too poor to retain counsel, the judge at this point assigns an attorney to defend the accused. If the accused pleads guilty at this time about all that remains is for the judge to set sentence. If the accused pleads not guilty, however, he is bound over for trial.

At the trial a jury which is acceptable to both prosecution and defense must first be selected. After jury selection, the prosecution opens the trial by making a general statement of charges following which a presentation of evidence, exhibits, and witnesses is made. The defense usually cross-examines each of the prosecution witnesses. After the prosecution's case is completed the defense ordinarily makes a motion for a directed verdict of acquittal claiming that insufficient evidence was presented by the prosecution. One of the basic tenets of American justice is that the burden of proof lies with the prosecution, and the judge must decide at this point whether the trial should continue or not.

If the motion for acquittal is denied, the defense presents its case attempting to illustrate further the insufficiency of the evidence presented by the prosecution. The accused may even waive his right to refuse to testify, and testify in his own behalf. An individual does not, however, have to testify and possibly thereby incriminate himself. After the defense finishes its case it may again move for dismissal of the charge.

After all the evidence and witnesses are presented by both sides and summation arguments by both sides have been made, the judge "charges" or instructs the jury with a general summary of the case and possible decisions that are available to the jury in the case. The jury retires to deliberate and must reach a unanimous decision in order for the accused individual to be convicted. If the jury finds the defendant not guilty he is immediately released. If the jury's verdict is guilty the defense may make a motion for a new trial and if this is denied the judge passes sentence on the convicted individual. In certain cases and for particular reasons or "errors," decisions may be appealed to the state supreme court.

Civil Cases

A civil suit ordinarily involves two private individuals in which the court is the mechanism through which the disputed issue is settled. If an individual feels he has been wronged by another he may file a formal complaint with the district court to which the defendant may file an answer. The person filing the complaint is the plaintiff and the individual against whom the complaint is filed is called the defendant.

The trial itself in a civil case is similar to that which takes place in a criminal case. If the subsequent decision is in favor of the plaintiff, court costs and damages, if any, as determined by the court, are paid by the defendant. Awarding of damages does not always insure payment, although the court might subsequently order payment through attachment of the defendant's wages or seizure of property.

SELECTION OF JUDGES

State court judges are selected in a variety of ways but the three most general methods of selection are: (1) popular election (34 states), either on nonpartisan or partisan tickets; (2) gubernatorial appointment (eleven states), either on a modified basis such as in Missouri or California, or strictly appointment by the governor with confirmation by the state senate such as in New Jersey; and, (3) legislative selection (5 states).

Wyoming has most recently changed its system for selecting judges to courts of general jurisdiction. Originally judges were elected to their positions on a partisan ballot, but from 1915 to 1972 district and supreme court judges were elected to these offices on a nonpartisan ballot. Following approval by the voters of a constitutional amendment in the 1972 election, all future vacancies on the Wyoming Supreme Court, the District Courts, and any other courts which might be brought within this system by the legislature will be filled under the "Merit Selection and Retention Plan," or as it is more popularly known, the "Missouri Plan." This plan, first adopted in Missouri in 1940, has the enthusiastic endorsement of the State Bar Association, the American Bar Association and the American Judicature Society.

Under the Missouri Plan[6] when vacancies occur through death, retirement, resignation, or desire not to run for reelection, it is the Governor who initially selects his replacement. The Governor, however, is restricted in his choice of a judge to a list of three qualified persons submitted to him by a special screening committee known as the Judicial Nominating Commission. The Governor must pick one of the three suggested individuals and has thirty days in which to make his choice or an appointment will be made by the Chief Justice of the Supreme Court.

The persons so nominated and appointed by the Governor serves in office for a minimum of one year. After this he must stand for retention in office for a full term (eight years for Supreme Court justices and six years for District Court judges) or for the unexpired portion of his predecessor's term. To be retained he must at the next general election receive the approval of a majority of the voters. There are no other candidates for the position. If the single candidate receives a majority he serves out the term; if he receives a negative vote the appointment process begins again with a list of three new names. At the end of a full term, a judge may decide to seek another full term. He must file a declaration to this effect and if he receives the approval of the Judicial Nominating Commission his name will be placed before the voters again for a new term. If the Judicial Nominating Commission refuses to allow the judge to seek voter approval a vacancy exists and another appointment must be made. This is a modification of the original Missouri Plan which is unique to Wyoming.

The Judicial Nominating Commission consists of seven members: Chief Justice of the Wyoming Supreme Court who is the chairman and votes only in the case of a tie; three practicing lawyers; and, three nonlawyers. The lawyers are elected by the State Bar Association and the nonlawyers are appointed by the Governor. No more than two residents of the same judicial district may serve on the commission at the same time.

For a great number of years much criticism has been levelled at the court systems of the various states, primarily centering around the "proper" method of selection of judges to various tribunals. The criticisms have been largely aimed at the popular elections of judges, a practice in operation in most of the states. One of the major arguments against popular election of judges has been that popular election puts the potential judge in a position of having to actively seek the position in a partisan or even nonpartisan political campaign for office, an activity, it is argued, that may seriously affect his subsequent impartiality on the bench if elected. Another argument suggests that the general public is not adequately equipped to assess the necessary qualifications required by a judge as a legal technician, plus the fact that the electorate is generally apathetic toward judicial elections. The American Bar Association and the various state bar associations have been suggesting for years that "better judges" would be obtained and retained if the judges were appointed rather than elected by popular vote or selected by the legislature. Appointment by the governor from a list of names selected by an "impartial" judicial council or the bar itself, the bar indicates, would remove the judges from partisan politics and assure the selection of competently trained and qualified judicial personnel.

Despite this controversy over the proper method of selection of judges, no appreciable differences can be noted among judges selected under the three major forms of judicial selection, concerning social background and political or judicial experience of the judges prior to their appointment.[7] As a matter of fact, in Wyoming many judges came to the bench through gubernatorial appointment in the first instance rather than winning their first term through the election process.

The legal qualifications for becoming a judge in Wyoming are relatively simple. Justices of the state supreme court must be 30 years of age, citizens of the United States, residents of the state for three years, trained in law with nine years of practice or previous judicial experience. District judges must be at least 28, a citizen, resident of the state for two years, and "learned in the law."[8]

These legal considerations, however, tell us little about the sociological and political prerequisites for becoming a judge no matter what the method of selection. Close examination of the backgrounds of state judges in the United States reveal some of the following social and political characteristics.[9] State judges, like congressmen and senators, tend to come from rural areas and small towns rather than from medium sized cities and large urban centers. Roughly half of the judges belong to what are classified as high-status religious groups. Judges, for the most part, are educated in their home states, especially in their legal education. Their education was for the most part in a state educational institution rather than in a prestigious Ivy League or in some other private educational institution. Judges, although devoting almost half of their careers to public service of one form or another, in their private practice have tended to come to the court with a small firm or independent practice background rather than either academic or corporation experience. Judges have spent a great deal of their adult life in public service, either partisan political activity or judicial activity—most of the judges had nearly as much public service as private experience. Nearly two-thirds of the judges surveyed indicated that they had served as either a county prosecuting attorney or a city attorney or both, usually early in their careers. The same number served in a lower judicial capacity prior to serving in their present positions. Thus, it should be evident that judges require more background than just the legal requirements set down by the state constitution.

LAW ENFORCEMENT

Closely related to the functioning of the state court system, especially with respect to criminal law, is the problem of law enforcement. For the most part, state government is responsible for enforcing the existing criminal laws in its jurisdiction since there is actually little national criminal law. The courts themselves do not enforce the law but only provide the mechanism through which cases are heard and the law is enforced. Therefore, in order to achieve an orderly society, it is necessary to establish official agencies charged with the responsibility for bringing violators of the law to justice.

At the head of the law enforcement machinery of the state is the governor. He has the primary responsibility for guiding and directing the efforts of the state in this regard. He commands the National Guard although this is an unwieldy mechanism for enforcing the law on a day-to-day basis. His chief legal advisor is the attorney general of the state whom he appoints. The attorney general has the primary responsibility for over-all coordination of law enforcement efforts in the state along with his advisory functions with regard to all state officials. There is no state police force as such, although the state highway patrol is responsible for enforcement of certain traffic laws in the state.

Most law enforcement activities are performed at the local level. Municipal police, town marshalls, county sheriffs, county prosecuting attorneys, and county coroners are responsible for performing these functions at the local level.

Except for city police and town marshalls, these officials are popularly elected on partisan ballots at the county level and operate, needless to say, somewhat independently. Thus law enforcement activities vary considerably according to the diligence and effort of many diverse and locally based officials, and the functioning of the courts in particular areas varies correlatively with local law enforcement activities.

Despite the local emphasis in law enforcement efforts, this activity illustrates vividly the importance of the federal sharing arrangement. In recent years, there has been a concerted effort by officials at all levels of government to overcome some of the problems created by numerous jurisdictional boundaries. Increased use of centralized record-keeping, mutual training facilities, fingerprint files, central crime detection laboratories, and communication networks, illustrate some of the cooperative measures being jointly adopted by law enforcement agencies at all levels of government.

FOOTNOTES

1. *United States Constitution,* Art. III, Sec. 2.
2. *Wyoming Constitution,* Art. V, Sec. 22.
3. *Ibid.,* Art. XIV, Secs. 1, 2.
4. A writ is an order of a court commanding the person to whom it is addressed to do or not to do some act. Quo warranto is a court order commanding a person to show by what authority he holds a particular position in government. Mandamus is a court order to an official of government commanding him to perform a certain non-discretionary act. Habeas corpus is a court order to a jailer to show cause for holding a prisoner. Review is a superior court revision of an order of a subordinate court. Prohibition is a writ issued by a superior court commanding a subordinate court to desist from proceeding in a matter outside of its jurisdiction. Certiorari is a writ from a superior court to a subordinate court directing that a certified record of its proceedings in a particular case be sent up for review.
5. *Wyoming Constitution,* Art. V, Sec. 3.
6. For a detailed discussion of this new plan with arguments for and against, see Michael J. Horan, *Choosing Judges in Wyoming: Popular Election or "Merit Selection"?* Laramie: Government Research Bureau, University of Wyoming, 1972.
7. Based on data obtained by the author from Charles Liebman, *Directory of American Judges,* Chicago: American Directories, A Corporation, 1955. These and following data in this section are contained in an unpublished paper by the author entitled "Justices of State Supreme Courts."
8. *Wyoming Constitution,* Art. V, Secs. 8, 12.
9. Computed from data in Liebman, *op. cit.*

CHAPTER SIX

Local Government

There are many other governments operating within the state's boundaries in addition to state government. Municipalities, counties, and numerous special districts of all sizes also operate in Wyoming. Legally, these local units of government are subject to state control, but in practice they operate quite independently. Because of this relative freedom from state control and direction in their day-to-day operations, local governments provide a boundary to the operations of the state political system.

The patterns and forms of local government have been changing considerably in recent years. Originally, the county was perhaps the most significant of local governments, operating essentially as an arm or arbitrary subdivision of the state. Before modern means of transportation and communication developed, the county provided the closest contact with government that an individual citizen had. With the decline of rural living, however, the city or municipality has become the center of local governmental concern. While Wyoming can hardly be classified as a heavily-populated metropolitan state, the nationwide trend toward urban living is nonetheless evident. In the 1940's less than 40 per cent of Wyoming's population lived in cities and towns of over 2,500 population. By 1950 the number of urban residents equalled the rural residents, and in the 1960 census, urban residents totaled 187,551, or about 56 per cent of the state's population. Actually another 13.5 per cent of the population lived in towns of less than 2,500 population making Wyoming's "urban" population around 70 per cent.

The importance of municipal government was enhanced in 1972 with the passage of the Home Rule amendment to the state constitution. This amendment provided that cities and towns could exempt themselves from the effects of legislation that was not uniform in its application to all the cities and towns. While this amendment did not make a major grant of power to the cities it did change the emphasis on city powers from a negative one to a positive approach. This point will be further discussed later in this chapter.

In addition to the increase in urban living, the number of special districts, excluding school districts, has grown considerably. As citizens demand more and more services and functions, many of which are beyond the capacity or desire of regular general governments to perform, special purpose districts are created to fulfill the demands or perform services.

The number of governments in Wyoming has actually declined in recent years despite the increase in the number of special districts. Because of consolidation and reorganization the number of school districts has steadily decreased. Besides the 23 counties in Wyoming and the 87 municipalities, there are 42 school districts and 185 special districts for a grand total of 339 governments (including the state and national governments) operating within the boundaries of the state. This means one governmental unit for every 980 people in the state.

Local governments not only exist in large numbers but their policies and taxes affect significantly the people in the state. Table 15 indicates the total amounts of property taxes for 1967 and 1973, including the small amount taken in from this source by the state government, and although property taxes are not the only source of income for local units of government, these taxes do make up the bulk of the intake of the local units. Not only is this much money taken in and spent, but local governments also supply over 15,000 local people with jobs. This is an increase of almost 100% over 20 years ago.

TABLE 15
Total Property Taxes by Purpose and Year in Wyoming

Purpose	1973	1967
Municipal	$ 3,141,527	$ 3,552,116
Schools and Colleges	72,787,731	45,428,539
County	14,984,219	11,734,782
Special Districts	2,837,048	1,141,406
State	0	2,927,163
Total	$93,750,525	$64,784,006

Source: Wyoming Taxpayers Association, *Wyoming Roundup: 1968 (1973) Tax Levies,* WTA, Report No. 369, September 1968 (No. 384, August 1973).

LEGAL STATUS OF LOCAL GOVERNMENTS

Local units of government in Wyoming and in the United States generally, are creatures of the state. The legal relationship between the state and local governments is of a unitary nature. Local governments have no inherent governmental powers, but have only expressed or delegated powers from the state, and those powers which can be reasonably implied from the enumerated powers. Specifically, the Wyoming constitution grants to the state legislature the power to provide for the creation and organization of counties and municipalities in the state.[1]

For legal purposes, local governmental units are public corporations, which means they enjoy continuous existence and such corporate rights as making contracts, suing and being sued, acquiring and disposing of property, borrowing, and exercising whatever other powers the state legislature may give to them. Although the legal distinction is sometimes blurred, the law generally classifies public corporations into two classes: municipal corporations and quasi-municipal corporations. The municipal corporation is truly a local agency of government having been created by and for local citizens with the approval and direction of the state, for purposes of providing certain desired services and functions permitted by law. Cities and towns are municipal corporations. While they are still "creatures" of the state, Wyoming's municipalities were granted in 1972 a measure of home rule through an amendment to the constitution approved by the electorate at the general election. This modifies the arbitrary power of the state over the municipalities. This will be discussed further below. On the other hand, local units of government such as counties, school districts, and special districts, are legally classified as quasi-municipal corporations, created by the state as administrative subdivisions for the accomplishment of state objectives such as law enforcement, assessment and collection of taxes, and provision of educational facilities.

MUNICIPAL GOVERNMENT

The general trend toward urbanization in this country has created numerous problems for governments at all levels. When people live in close proximity to one another, they have need for various services that under rural conditions are not necessary or can be provided individually. In densely populated areas, however, many required services are best provided through government rather than by individual effort. The municipal form of government is created to meet the needs of urban living.

The primary functions of municipalities thus are closely related to the service needs created by urbanization. Although the number and extent of municipal functions is directly related to the size of the urban area, some of the more common services and functions of cities and towns in Wyoming are: protective services such as fire, police, and public health protection; street construction and maintenance; sanitation including dumps, refuse collection, sewage collection and disposal; parks and recreation facilities; municipal water supplies.[2] In addition some cities have public cemeteries, public hospitals, municipal airports, golf courses, municipal electric utilities, and many other public facilities and buildings for citizen use.

The governmental structures through which these various services and functions are performed take at least three different forms in the 90 Wyoming cities and towns.[3] The state statutes provide for the following three forms of municipal government: mayor-council, council manager, and commission governments. The statutes have, in the past, also provided for a commission-manager form although no city had ever adopted this form in Wyoming and it was deleted in the new municipal code of 1965. No city presently uses the commission form.

Mayor-Council Government

The most prevalent form of city government used in Wyoming and in the United States as a whole, is the mayor-council form. Under this system, which in some ways is comparable to the separation of powers at the state and national levels, the elective council is primarily the policy-determining body, while the elective mayor is technically the city's chief executive.

The number of individuals on the council varies in cities of the United States and even in Wyoming cities and towns, depending upon their size. In towns (less than 4,000 population) four councilmen and a mayor are elected. The council members are elected for four-year terms and the mayor for a two-year term. In first-class cities of Wyoming the size of the council is variable. In these cities the council must divide the city into at least three wards of not less than 1,000 population each and also determine whether two or three council members will be elected from each of the created wards. The voters in each ward elect to four-year terms two or three councilmen for that ward. In first-class cities, the mayor is elected at large by the voters to a four-year term.

Governmental powers are delegated to the council by the state legislature. The new municipal code of Wyoming (1965) lists 39 specific grants of power to city councils, and, in addition, grants all other powers "deemed necessary for the health, safety, or welfare of the city," or necessary to carry out the specific grants of power. These specific grants of power are related primarily to (1) financial authority such as taxation, appropriation of funds, and borrowing, and (2) regulatory powers relating to such diverse matters as zoning, traffic control, health, and building codes. These general powers are held by the governing bodies of cities whether under mayor-council, manager, or commission form of government. The home rule amendment liberalized these functions somewhat.

The mayor presides and has voting rights in all council meetings and generally controls all administrative affairs of the municipality. In towns, the mayor appoints, and may remove for certain reasons, a town clerk, treasurer, and marshall. In first-class cities the city clerk, treasurer, engineer, attorney, fire chief, police chief, policemen, and police justices are appointed and may be removed by the mayor, subject to certain conditions specified by the council. Further, in first-class cities, the mayor is entitled to sign or veto any ordinance passed by the city council. His veto may be overruled by the city council by a two-thirds vote of all the elected members. His veto power also includes an item veto on any items in appropriation ordinances. The mayor also from time to time must "communicate to the governing body such information and recommend such measures as in his opinion may tend to improve the finances of the city, the police, health, comfort and general prosperity of the city."[4]

Finally, it should be noted that the mayor-council form of government existing in Wyoming is the "strong mayor" type. In many other states the mayor is in a very "weak" administrative position. In many cases, department heads are either popularly elected or mayoral appointments are subject to strict council control. Also, the mayor does not necessarily prepare the budget and often has little control over the administrative affairs of the city. This is not the case in Wyoming cities and towns.

Council-Manager Government

Two of Wyoming's largest cities—Laramie and Casper—have a council-manager form of city government. Under this system, the council has roughly the same functions as it does under the mayor-council form. The council is responsible for the legislative or policy-making functions of city government, passing ordinances and resolutions concerning necessary policy matters. In addition, the council hires a city manager and holds him responsible for the administration and execution of governmental policies. The mayor is retained under this form but his duties are primarily ceremonial. He is chosen from the membership of the city council, presides over council meetings, and has various other ceremonial functions such as dedications, ribbon cuttings, issuing proclamations, and buying the first poppy.

In Wyoming the size of the council varies with the size of the city. In cities and towns having a population of less than 4,000 there are three councilmen; those cities with a population between 4,000 and 20,000 have seven council members; and cities over 20,000 with council-manager government, there are nine council members. Council members may be chosen by wards or at large, whichever method is preferred by the city adopting this particular form.

The city manager is hired by the council for an indefinite period and is responsible to it. As head of the administrative departments of the city, the manager is responsible for: (1) executing and enforcing city ordinances; (2) appointing, supervising, and possibly removing city personnel; (3) making policy recommendations and reports to the council; (4) preparing and submitting a budget of proposed income and expenditures to the council; and, (5) performing all duties imposed on him by the council.

The advantages of manager government claimed by its proponents are many, although some drawbacks are also evident. Supposedly, the city manager is a full-time, well-trained, well-paid, nonpolitical central executive who creates in the city administration a business-like atmosphere. His professional competence and full-time devotion to the job is often contrasted to part-time commissioners or mayors, not trained specifically for meeting city problems. Theoretically, the government supplied under a manager is free from partisan politics, thus raising standards, reducing waste, and saving money.

The advantages of the city manager form of government are, however, often over-evaluated. Mere adoption of this form does not automatically insure "good government." Politics exist in city governments no matter what the form, even though partisan Democratic and Republican politics may not exist in name.

Also, it is often pointed out that under a manager there may be a lack of real responsible political leadership usually characteristic of mayor-council forms. The manager is not supposed to be the policy leader and the city council has generally not assumed its responsibilities of political leadership. Finally, city managers, because of legal residence requirements, often are local individuals not trained specifically for the job.

In summary, there are several important characteristics of the council-manager form of government: (1) there is a relatively small council with general legislative powers and policy-making prerogatives as outlined by the state legislature; (2) the council hires a professional city manager for an indefinite period and can remove him; (3) the manager is responsible to the council for the administration, appointment, removal, and direction of administrative personnel; and, (4) the manager prepares and submits to the council the budget and other recommendations for their approval.

Commission Government

Another form of city government in the United States is the commission form. Under this system the only elective officers of the city are commissioners, elected at large on a nonpartisan ballot. These commissioners perform both executive and legislative functions, ordinarily performed by separate branches of government. Collectively, the commissioners, ranging in number from three to seven, are the city council or legislative and policy-making body; individually, each commissioner heads a specific department of city government. One of the commissioners serves as mayor although he does not have ordinary executive prerogatives and his powers are no greater than either of the other commissioners. The mayor under the commission form serves largely in a ceremonial and titular capacity. Currently no Wyoming city uses this option. Cheyenne for many years operated with the commission form but in 1971 switched to the mayor-council form.

City Politics

One of the most significant features of city politics is that reformers have been able to remove municipal elections from the partisan framework. To be sure politics exist in cities but in a different form, since elections to posts of mayor, council, or commissioner are on a nonpartisan basis. Until 1963, all municipal elections in Wyoming were even held at a different time than regular partisan contests. Town elections are still conducted in May rather than November, but elections in first-class cities currently are held during the general November elections.

Nonpartisan elections seem to have had some effects on the type of politics that exists in the jurisdictions that use them. Since political parties are not formally involved, other groups such as chambers of commerce or service clubs have somewhat more influence. There is less campaigning and personal characteristics of the candidates seem to be emphasized. Although the partisan struggle between Democrats and Republicans is at a minimum in city affairs, the political struggle still exists.

The political problems of city governments are to a large extent the same as those of other levels of government. There is a struggle over the distribution of goods, both material and symbolic; some people are advantaged while others are deprived. Professor Thompson, in his analysis of municipal finances, lists the following as representative of problems faced by Wyoming municipalities: increasing population with a corresponding demand for more services; increasing standard of living; inflation in service and salary costs; backlog of needs left over from the depression and two wars; technological advances such as the automobile which have increased the need for bigger and better streets and increased measures of traffic control; and, problems created by an inadequate revenue base.[5] Within the cities some groups are demanding more and better services while others are not convinced that cities are even necessary much less that they should provide such frivolities as parks and recreation.

Further, the city must compete in the larger state and national political arenas for the tax dollar. Competition among educators, county officials, state officers, and municipal leaders is growing more intense as resources become more scarce and demands become greater. Some cities are even going to Washington with their problems which have been long ignored at the state level. Cities often have been far more successful in their appeals for aid to the national government than they have been at the state level. The city then is part of the larger political game often attempting to play the state off against the national government.

Two factors already mentioned in other connections will have a tremendous impact on local governments in Wyoming—home rule and revenue sharing. In November 1972 voters approved an amendment to the state constitution providing for some measure of local determination of local affairs in the municipalities of the state. While there are several significant exceptions to this grant, the amendment provides a positive element to municipal programs. Municipalities are no longer restricted to specific grants of authority from the legislature but are encouraged to use innovation and imagination in providing services and programs for their citizens. Significant exceptions to home rule ordinances are civil service provisions, retirement, collective bargaining, levying of taxes, excises, fees, or other charges. All cities and towns within these limits are empowered to determine their local affairs and government through charter ordinances subject to popular referendum and further subject to uniform statutes subsequently passed by the state legislature. If state statutes are not uniform throughout the state and for all classes of municipalities, a city or town may choose to exempt itself from the provisions of the state statute. It can accomplish this by a charter ordinance passed by a two-thirds vote of all members elected to the governing body of the city or town. Charter ordinances do not take effect for 60 days after passage. If during the waiting period 10 per cent of the number of voters at the last municipal election sign a petition demanding that the ordinance be subjected to referendum, the council must hold a referendum on the ordinance within 90 days. The charter ordinance takes effect if a majority of the electors voting on the issue approve. Certainly this home rule provision is not earth shattering in its scope or grant of power but it does provide a positive note to city affairs. The last section of the authorizing constitutional amendment provides that "the powers and authority granted to cities and towns . . . shall be liberally construed for the purpose of giving the largest measure of self-government to cities and towns."

Revenue sharing, of course, will have a significant impact on the financial affairs of both municipalities and counties in the state. While the dollar amount is not extremely large it will enable local units of government to accomplish many worthwhile projects which have previously been just beyond their capabilities. Revenue sharing also allows the units to accomplish these objectives without significant debt or increased taxes. Perhaps local units will become program oriented rather than tax oriented.

COUNTY GOVERNMENT

The state constitution has little to say about the organization and governing of its subdivisions, counties, other than that the legislature has power to provide for organizing new counties and "such officers as may be necessary."[6] Counties, like cities, are subdivisions of the state and as such are legally and politically dependent upon the state. The county is created by the state legislature, derives its powers from and is responsible to the state. Unlike cities there is often considerable state administrative direction and control over county functions particularly with regard to highways and roads, finances, personnel, health and welfare, and education. Counties, therefore, have limited powers and may engage only in such functions as are authorized by the constitution and/or the legislature. Counties may levy taxes and borrow money to carry out designated functions with specified limits on amounts in the constitution. Unlike cities, counties are not even able to determine the form of government desired, nor even to specify the required number of officials. In general then, the county is primarily a state subdivision with local officials in charge of state programs.

Compared with governments on the national and state level, county government seems to be somewhat disorganized. There is not the separation of powers between the legislature and administration characteristic of state and national governments, but rather a vast array of general officers, specific positions, partisan and nonpartisan positions, most of whom are elected individually by the citizens of the county and none of whom are necessarily responsible to any other. Generally speaking, county officers in Wyoming can be divided into two broad categories: (1) the governing board, and, (2) other elective officers with specific functions.

County Governing Boards

The general governing body of Wyoming counties is the board of county commissioners. Three commissioners are elected at large from the county to four-year staggered terms. In contrast to other county officials, county commissioners are only part-time officials meeting only periodically during the year. One of the commissioners is designated as chairman of the board. Although the county board is the "legislative" body of county government, it possesses very few actual legislative powers. Most of the board's legislative powers concern fiscal affairs of the county. Subject to constitutional and legislative limitations, the board levies and apportions taxes, provides for capital improvements, borrows money, and makes appropriations. The board also has some regulatory functions to perform such as control over sale of liquor in the county outside municipal boundaries. County boards do not define crimes and fix penalties or determine rights and duties of citizens. Again, the county is primarily an administrative subdivision of the state.

Most of the functions of the board of county commissioners are of an executive nature. The board is responsible for supervising, building, and maintaining county roads; purchasing and maintaining county buildings and property; establishing election precincts; purchasing and distributing office supplies for other county officials; equalizing taxes; and, performing other similar administrative duties.

Other County Officers

In most states, including Wyoming, there are from eight to 15 other major county officials, usually elected by popular vote and relatively independent from supervision by either the board of county commissioners or the state. In Wyoming there are seven such officials: clerk, treasurer, assessor, sheriff, attorney, coroner, and clerk of district court. All are elected to four-year terms on partisan ballots. In contrast to the board of county commissioners these officials serve in a full-time capacity.

The county clerk is primarily responsible for keeping records of various kinds such as land titles and transfers, mortgages, automobile registration, marriage licenses, and vital statistics. He is also secretary to the board of county commissioners, and purchasing agent and chief budget officer of the county. Finally, the clerk is responsible for the conduct of elections in the county.

There are four county officers in Wyoming who are closely related to judicial processes and law enforcement in the state: county attorney, clerk of district court, sheriff, and coroner. The county attorney is not only the official legal advisor of the county board and other county officials on their legal questions, powers, and duties, but he represents the state in criminal cases as the prosecuting attorney. Since grand juries are rarely, if ever, used in this state, it is within the discretion of the prosecuting attorney whether to vigorously enforce the laws or practically negate them by refusing to prosecute. As the name implies the clerk of district court is the chief administrative officer of the district court for his county. The clerk keeps court records of civil, criminal, and probate cases, special districts, adoptions, and workman's compensation.

The county sheriff is found in all states and is not only a county but also a state official. He is the principal peace officer in the county; an officer of the district court for issuing summons, warrants, and executing judgments; custodian of the county jail and prisoners; and, performer of various other miscellaneous duties such as collecting delinquent taxes and disposing of property for failure to pay taxes. The most important present-day function of the county coroner is to hold inquests to determine, if possible, the cause of any death occurring by violent means or under suspicious circumstances.

There are two county officials concerned primarily with taxing and finances in the county. The county treasurer is responsible for collecting revenue, custody of county funds, paying county bills, and keeping the financial records of the county. The county assessor is responsible for valuation of real and personal property in the county. The assessor prepares the county tax roll for the treasurer based on his assessment of each piece of personal and real property in the county.

County governmental structure has been heavily criticized for its disorganization, diffusion of responsibility, large numbers of elective officers, and poor administrative procedures. Undoubtedly there are some improvements that might be made, but county officials are not likely to instigate or favor massive reorganization. Historical precedent and tradition seem to favor the local court house and its present system of organization.

SPECIAL DISTRICTS

In addition to counties and municipalities in Wyoming, there is another state governmental subdivision that deserves mention although it is often overlooked. This is known as the special district, created ordinarily to perform a particular service that some individuals desire. In the states generally, including Wyoming, there has been a trend toward increased establishment and use of the special purpose district to accomplish specific governmental functions that are not performed by the general purpose governmental units such as counties or municipalities.

There are a number of reasons why the special district device has received increased consideration and use.[7] In the first place the special district is often used where a service area is somewhat smaller than existing jurisdictions such as counties or the proposed service area crosses county boundaries. Secondly, in other cases, existing governmental units are not able to perform a particular desired service because of financial or functional limitations. There are constitutional and legislative restrictions on city and county tax and debt limits which often preclude financing certain new services or functions. Also, functional restrictions by the legislature on general governments may prevent their involvement in certain programs demanded by citizens. Third, general governments may be administratively unable to assume new service responsibilities or may not desire to do so for political reasons. They may even encourage special district establishment for these reasons, thus opening the door for the creation of a special district. Fourth, the desire for "grass roots" control and political independence of established governments undoubtedly is an important reason for establishing special districts. Finally, functional specialization and the relative ease of establishing districts seem to be important. Districts can be set up relatively quickly and in the age of specialization, technicians and specialists have used the special district device for establishing a service quickly and without the need to convince general governmental officials.

Special districts exist in a variety of forms and sizes in the United States, and perform services of almost every conceivable type. In Wyoming, the following types of special districts exist or have existed in the past: school, community college, weed and pest control, fire protection, hospital, cemetery, sanitary and improvement, water and sewer, irrigation, public irrigation and power, drainage, soil and water conservation, water conservancy, predatory animal, district health departments, and local improvement assessment districts. Also the legislature has authorized procedures for establishing power districts, revenue bond power districts, livestock districts, dog control districts, in addition to permitting county government to establish special boards and commissions for such functions as libraries, county hospitals, fairgrounds, airports, and parks. Excluding school districts and local special assessment districts, the United States Census Bureau in 1962 found 144 special districts in Wyoming.[8]

Creation and Structure of Special Districts

Although the specific procedure for establishing special districts varies according to the district involved, even in Wyoming, there are a few general points that might be mentioned regarding the creation of a district. The state legislature, of course, must have passed a general enabling statute providing for the establishment of a particular kind of district. Normally the first step in the process is the circulation of a petition in the area concerned. With a specified number of signatures, the petition is then presented to certain legally designated officials such as the district court judge, for example. The responsibility of the agency or official receiving the petition varies, but he may be required to hold a hearing on the proposed district or at least notify through publication, residents of the area of a pending decision in this regard. Ordinarily, the next step is to hold an election in which residents of the proposed district are allowed to indicate their desires on the issue.

The governing bodies of special districts are always some form of board or commission. Usually, there are three to five members and, in Wyoming, these individuals are ordinarily elected from the district, although county commissioners or other similar officials may appoint some board members such as fair boards or airport boards, for example. In certain types of special districts, voting for officers is limited to land or property owners in the district. Legislative statutes determine the powers which are believed necessary to accomplish the purpose or goals of the district. Normally, the board has power to use eminent domain; acquire property; levy taxes or special assessments; borrow money; authorize expenditures; and, contract for services and/or materials to be used by the district employees or officers. On the other hand, soil conservation districts ordinarily do not have the power to tax or borrow, but must rely often on cooperative agreements and contributions from other local districts, state or national government. A district board is also usually responsible for hiring and directing activities and work of any personnel that may be necessary to accomplish the work of the district.

Because there is no mention of special districts in the constitution, questions concerning the legal status of districts and limitations on their powers have arisen. Whereas counties and municipalities are constitutionally restricted in terms of tax and debt limits, the constitution is not clear regarding special districts. In at least two cases the Wyoming supreme court has attempted to straighten out this problem. In one case the court indicated that the bonded indebtedness limitations applying to cities and towns also applied to special districts rendering quasi-municipal functions.[9] In another case the court indicated that constitutional tax rate limitations applied to special districts if they were performing a quasi-municipal function—in this case fire protection—but otherwise the limitations did not apply as, for example, in cemetery and hospital districts.[10] In the former case, the court strongly suggested that the constitution should be clarified in regard to these matters, but no action has subsequently been taken by the legislature.

In summary, trends in the establishment and use of special districts should be noted. School districts have generally been on the decline in terms of numbers. Many states, including Wyoming, have been engaged in consolidation movements in recent years resulting in decreased numbers of school districts. In relation to other types of special districts, however, the trend throughout the United States has been toward increased use of this device for providing particular services and functions. Wyoming also has experienced an increased use of special districts and this trend is likely to continue in the near future. Proliferation of special districts can cause a great amount of duplication and overlapping of functions, not to mention the tax burden which might be imposed by numerous districts on an individual citizen. It is possible, for example, that a rural farm owner might be included in a drainage, school, cemetery, fire, hospital, irrigation, water conservancy, soil and water conservation, district health department, community college, and weed and pest control district. An urban resident also might be included in a number of the above districts in addition to street construction and maintenance, recreation, paving, lighting and similar special assessment districts in his municipality.

FOOTNOTES

1. *Wyoming Constitution,* Art. XII, Sec. 2; Art. XIII, Sec. 1.
2. See John T. Thompson, Vincent V. Picard, Samuel L. Anderson, *Municipal Finance in Wyoming,* Laramie: Adult Education and Community Services, University of Wyoming, 1964, pages 53-55.
3. Municipalities over 4,000 population are classified as first-class cities. These include Cheyenne, Casper, Laramie, Sheridan, Rock Springs, Rawlins, Riverton, Worland, Evanston, Cody, Powell, Newcastle, Torrington, and Lander. All other municipal corporations in the state are towns.
4. *Wyoming Statutes,* 1957, 15-56.
5. Thompson, *et al., op. cit.,* pages 8-11.
6. *Wyoming Constitution,* Art. XII, Secs. 2, 5.
7. Joseph Geraud, *Special Taxing Districts in Wyoming,* Wyoming Legislative Research Committee, Research Report No. 5, December, 1960, Chapter 1.
8. Bureau of the Census, *Census of Governments: 1962,* Volume 1, Washington, D.C.: U.S. Government Printing Office, 1963, page 371.
9. *In Re West Sanitary and Improvement District,* 77 Wyo 384, (1957).
10. *War Memorial Hospital vs. Board of County Commissioners,* 73 Wyo. 371 (1955).